ASK
AND YOU WILL
SUCCEED

ASK
AND YOU WILL
SUCCEED

1001 Extraordinary Questions to Create Life-Changing Results, Revised and Updated

KENNETH D. FOSTER

WILEY

John Wiley & Sons, Inc.

Published by John Wiley & Sons, Inc., Hoboken, New Jersey.
Published simultaneously in Canada.

For general information on our other products and services or for technical support, please contact our Customer Care Department within the United States at (800) 762-2974, outside the United States at (317) 572-3993 or fax (317) 572-4002.

Wiley also publishes its books in a variety of electronic formats. Some content that appears in print may not be available in electronic books. For more information about Wiley products, visit our web site at www.wiley.com.

Library of Congress Cataloging-in-Publication Data:

Foster, Ken D., 1951-

Ask and you will succeed : 1001 extraordinary questions to create life-changing results/ by Kenneth D. Foster. — Rev. and updated.

    p. cm.

    ISBN 978-0-470-45593-7 (cloth)

    1. Success—Psychological aspects. 2. Self-actualization (Psychology) I. Title.

BF637.S8F637 2009

650.1—dc22

                             2008052086

Printed in the United States of America

10 9 8 7 6 5 4 3 2 1

To my beloved friend, and mentor, Parmahansa
Yogananda, and all who seek wisdom and the power to realize
their true nature, unleash their full potential, and bring forth
unending success in this world and in the afterworld

CONTENTS

SECTION 1
QUESTIONS FOR THE BIG PICTURE

SECTION 2
QUESTIONS TO GROW YOUR POTENTIAL

SECTION 3
QUESTIONS TO BRING YOU WHAT YOU WANT

SECTION 4
QUESTIONS TO CREATE FINANCIAL FREEDOM

SECTION 5
QUESTIONS TO EMPOWER
YOUR CONNECTIONS

SECTION 6
QUESTIONS TO PROMOTE WELL-BEING

SECTION 7
QUESTIONS THAT WILL GIVE YOU MORE JOY

SECTION 8
THE ONLY REMAINING QUESTIONS

ACKNOWLEDGMENTS

I would first like to humbly acknowledge my Creator and the loving presence that comes through my writings and writes all the scripts in life, the spiritual source of creation within all of us. The gifts that have been bestowed on me by this divine presence are too numerous to list, so I have found that by living in the presence daily and carving my own beautiful life sculpture, I have become the gift I once sought.

I would like to thank my teachers and guides, seen and unseen, that have guided me through the maze of life and protected me from harm's way in all of my affairs. I would also like to acknowledge my sincere love for the thousands of people who have passed through my life. Whether my closest friends, family, casual acquaintance, enemies, or someone just passing by—each one of you has shown up in my life at exactly the perfect time and place to teach me what I sought or needed to learn. Each and every one of you has brought me untold gifts of wisdom, healing, compassion, laughter, joy, and love. For that, I am eternally grateful.

I would like to thank my mother Edith, my father Donald Foster, sister Kathleen Munz, and brothers Kevin and Kirk Foster, who have given me the gift of unconditional love and the space to ask new questions. I would like to acknowledge my daughters Brooke, Erica, and Tara and all of my family members whose presence in my life has given me unending inspiration and the courage to pursue greater dreams. And most importantly, I wish to express my deep gratitude and appreciation to my best friend and loving wife, Judy, for her unending compassion, patience, guidance, and love.

I would also like to express my profound gratitude to my agent, Bill Gladstone, the team at John Wiley & Sons, Inc., and all those who directly or indirectly contributed to this project, including Sharon Lindenburger, Michelle Stimson, Camille Hughes, John Rudin, Autumn Lew, Erin Saxton, Kristen Loberg, Bob Korman, Dr. John Neyman, Jack Canfield, Steve Sorkin, Lori Wagner, Gerry Moore, Kasey Zanolli, John Assaraf, Peggy McCall, Debbie Ford, Arielle Ford, Gregory Scott Reid, Marci Shimoff, Gay Hendricks, Mitch Mortimer, Mark Victor Hansen, T. Harv Ecker, Robert Allen, Bob Proctor, Eric Lofholm, Jill Lublin, Cynthia

Kersey, Anthony Robbins, Bill Bartmann, Bob Scheinfield, Alex Mandossian, Steven E. Schmidt, Mari Smith, Paul DeKleermaeker, Jill Haans, Guy Lyman, Eric Buxton, Linda Woods, Arvee Robinson, Lee Pound, Austin Vickers, Mick Moore, Rick Fishman, Paul Freedman, Stephanie Hartman, Stephanie Crowley, Rand Pip, Ellen Steifler, David Metzler, Robert Grant, Ted Nevels, Brian Tracy, Cheryl Richardson, Ray DuGray, Maria Ngo, Melanie Benson Strict, Therese Skelly, Mary Pat Cavanaugh, Judi Bryan, Gary, Christie, and Donna Knight, Chuck Douglas, David Riklan, Scott Martineau, Joe Crump, Terry Levine, Sharon Wilson, Declan Dunn, and the Shared Vision Network Affiliates, my coaching clients and audiences who have taught me, and all the unnamed people who have helped me bring forth this work, you know who you are. I appreciate all of you and thank you for helping me bring this work into the world.

FOREWORD

Ken Foster has done it! This book has the power to change your business and your life. There is no book on the market like this one. Through his studies of human behavior and the mind, Ken has come across the simple—yet profound—formula to tap into higher realms of consciousness using the power of questions. This book will feed you mentally, emotionally, physically, and spiritually, by showing you the way to use your mind in obtaining what is most important for you.

Through Ken's simple method he will show you how to focus your mind like never before. As a result, you will tap into the hidden strength within you and find the answers to your greatest challenges, avoid new disasters, and bridge the gap from where you currently are to manifesting your greatest dreams. Ken is the master thinker. When it comes to teaching people to go within and ask the right questions, no one else can touch him. He is the Socrates of our time.

The pace of life is too frantic for many people, like being in a bad movie that won't stop. They are working more hours than ever, worried about their futures, concerned about the planet, juggling finances, and trying to keep up with massive amounts of information bombarding them on a daily basis. Many people carry a tremendous burden of guilt because they feel unsuccessful and are unhappy—discontent with their life. That is not the way to live! Can you relate to this? There is a growing need for people to balance their life and take back control. *Ask and You Will Succeed* will help you do this in many ways. And the benefits apply whether you are a CEO, corporate employee, entrepreneur, or homemaker.

The more sweetener you put into water, the sweeter it becomes. Likewise, the better the questions you ask, the sweeter your life will become. As I read, with fascination, the questions in each category, I found myself instantly asking and applying the questions to ongoing projects and relationships of my own. Therein is the great value of this book. You can instantly ask a new question and change your focus and direction immediately. The questions in each category are asked in such a way to affect your thinking at once.

I've asked on many occasions over the years, "What can I do to help more people live an incredible life?" This has probably been the most asked question of me throughout my career. *The Success Principles,* the *Chicken Soup for the Soul* series, *The Power of Focus, The Aladdin Factor, Dare to Win, Maximum Confidence, Self-Esteem and Peak Performance, Heart at Work and Peak Performance,* which have sold millions of copies, have all been focused on answering that question. So, when Ken asked me to write the foreword to his book, I looked to see if this book will help more people live an incredible life. The answer is an overwhelming yes, because it helps people form the habit of introspection.

Introspection is the key to living an extraordinary life. If you can look at yourself or your business dispassionately and recognize that you have faults and weaknesses, then you can change. People who don't analyze circumstances never change and rarely succeed in the areas of life that matter most. Ken has provided the categories and the right questions to help you take stock of what is happening in your world. When you go to bed each night, review your day and go over your experiences. How did I react today? Did I empower others? Did I meet my goals? Where did I let myself, or others down? What areas can I improve upon? Did I use self-control when the situations were irritating? Ask introspective questions and your life will get better.

This book helps fight the battle of scarcity thinking. Ken Foster knows far too well the ravages of wrong thinking and asking the wrong questions. He lost all his possessions twice in his life, but he pulled himself out of it. His results speak for themselves. He knows we are here to live life fully, to live it abundantly, to find joy in what we are doing and to use our mind to expand and magnify our lives. He has given you the key to unlock the life you have always wanted.

The key is one that you already hold, but may not be using effectively. It is the key to success that the prophets, spiritual leaders, and inspirational speakers have tried to tell us for thousands of years. Success is not about looking outside yourself for something that you don't have, but rather reaching inside to find what is already there. Your level of personal fulfillment, prosperity, success, and financial wealth can be traced back to the questions you ask and the actions you take on a daily basis. Ken Foster has dedicated his life to coaching others and helping them tap in to their inner compass to success. And he will teach you that anything is possible . . . if you dare to ask!

The success I have enjoyed can be traced back to the questions I asked. I have dreamed big and asked big questions over the years, which have resulted in unending success. You can too, by asking the questions found in *Ask and You Will Succeed*.

—Jack Canfield
coauthor, *Chicken Soup for the Soul*

INTRODUCTION

When many people think about success, their thoughts almost inevitably turn toward career, business, and finances. In today's society, we place a very high value on career and business success since we spend so much of our lives in the workplace. However, as important as your business success is, it's not the whole story of your life. In fact, there are those who would say that true success is really about our deepest values, and not just about the externals. And furthermore, your business, career, and financial success are hugely influenced by the success you have in other aspects of your life—your health, your relationships, your spirituality, your life purpose, and many other life experiences that don't have anything directly to do with money but which nevertheless determine whether we are truly rich or not.

We see many driven businesses and time-squeezed high-pressure entrepreneurs out there. They may have achieved enormous financial and professional success, but when we look closer, we see that their lives are gravely out of balance. Almost inevitably when such a driven person reaches mid-life or beyond, questions arise in that person's psyche, such as "Is that all there is to my life?," "How come I have so much but I still don't feel happy?," and "Everyone says I'm successful and my bank account says that too, but why don't I *feel* successful?"

You may be an individual who's been attempting to establish yourself in business and it's just not going the way you want it to. You might say to yourself, "I'm trying really hard, nothing is working out. I didn't get the promotion, the bank turned me down for financing, I'm never in the right place at the right time." Chances are that the obstacles you're encountering only *appear* to be external. The *real* obstacles preventing you from achieving your goals are *inside* you, and until you find them and root them out, success will continue to elude you.

True success is success in *all* parts of your life. You certainly want to achieve the highest business and professional success you're capable of, but you also want to be happy, feel in tune with your life purpose, have fulfilling relationships, and a spirituality that connects with the larger web of life all around you. I wrote this book to help you explore all the realms of your life.

The method I have used—a system of searching and provocative questions on all the topics in the book—is a tradition thousands of years old. The great Greek philosopher Socrates, who lived from 469 B.C. to 399 B.C., was renowned for teaching his students by asking them questions. Whenever a student brought up a subject for exploration, Socrates would not answer the student's questions. Instead he asked the *student* a question about the question, and upon receiving an answer, asked the student *another* question about that answer. According to legend, this process could go on for hours.

Imagine some of the initial frustration Socrates' students might have experienced when the master would not answer their questions directly but instead forced them to explore their own issues by tackling the questions themselves! Socrates knew, and his students soon learned, that the answer to life's most pressing questions do not dwell in some outside authority, but instead *within* each human being. This method of teaching by questions has come to be known (not surprisingly) as the Socratic Method.

I give the Socratic Method my own particular twist in this book, which evolved over the last 14 years of working with hundreds of individual coaching clients and through my own self-exploration. In its classic form, the Socratic Method involves the use of questions to create a dialogue between a teacher and a student. Here, in these pages, you *will* be having a dialogue, but not with an external teacher. You'll be dialoguing with yourself, but not with just the surface level of yourself. These questions are designed to take you deeper. You will be exploring realms of consciousness that are rarely explored by most people. You'll be peering into your subconscious and superconscious mind to bring forth your inner truth, wisdom, and intuition. You'll be asking yourself the questions in each section, and then answering yourself, then asking more questions, then answering more questions. You will be teaching yourself about life—*your* life—by asking yourself these extraordinary questions. You will be your own Socrates.

The questions are specifically designed to help you discover the values, beliefs, and rules by which you are currently living and to help you create quantum breakthroughs in the areas of business, finance, career, health, relationship, family, spirituality, and more.

Believe it, at this very moment you are capable of amazing improvement in all areas of your life. Your innate power is waiting to be realized and by following the step-by-step formula for asking and answering specific questions, you will tap into that power. You will find wealth in all areas of life. You'll discover what you need to achieve success in business. You will greatly enrich your relationships. You will deeply connect with your spirit. You will significantly enhance your personal effectiveness and achieve harmonious balance, happiness, and fulfillment. Yes, you will do this and much more by understanding how your mind works and then by simply asking the right questions, connecting with your inner truth and following through with daily actions.

We live in an abundant universe where there is no shortage of anything. Look around! In truth, there is no shortage of food, water, money, clothing, housing, love, or happiness. It is everywhere! But, as Socrates knew thousands of years ago and we still know *now*, there is a shortage of right thinking. Why do some nations have so much and others have so little? It all comes down to how we use our minds and how we distribute our resources. We've often gotten off track. There are many reasons for this. The primary reason, however, is that there is a shortage of wisdom, compassion, creativity, focus, and discipline.

Albert Einstein was quite ordinary in many ways. He did have one extraordinary quality, however—the ability to engage in disciplined contemplation. He had a unique way of focusing his mind. He asked himself searching, deep, and even sometimes whimsical questions to open up his creativity. By asking himself, "What would it look like to ride a light beam?," he conjured up what is now known as the Special Theory of Relativity and his most famous equation, $E = mc^2$ (which he claimed came to him in a dream, no doubt percolating in his psyche from the questions he was asking). The powerful questions he asked changed the history of physics and how we look at our universe. You can do the same!

Why do so many people just settle instead of creating a life filled with an abundance of love, happiness, and wealth? Because most unsuccessful people live life from the outside in, rather than the inside out. They are driven by their baggage instead of being inspired by their soul. They listen to the opinions, advice, and counsel of others instead of taking time to realize what is real, valuable, and right for them. Eventually, living this way causes their dreams to die, their visions to wither, and they get stuck in mediocrity—just hanging in there listening to what others think is best for them.

On the other hand, those who take time for honest introspection notice the patterns of their life. They have respect for themselves and take care of themselves. They review who they are becoming by their actions or nonactions. They look at what is working or not and make adjustments with a positive attitude. They know that everything counts and they take full responsibility for their actions and their lives. These individuals are the truth seekers, ever looking at improving their life and making a difference in the world.

To change the conditions of your life, you must become aware of the way you are using your mind. From the moment we open our eyes in the morning until we close our eyes at night and drift to sleep, our minds are filled with thoughts passing through our consciousness. Where do these thoughts come from? We are like radio receivers—we tune in and attract certain thoughts just like tuning in to a radio station brings you the music or news being played by that station. The top quantum scientists, neuroplasticity scientists, ancient religious texts, and great spiritual leaders of our time all concur that thought comes to us by the use of our brain and by the focused power of the mind. The new thought of today is "Train Your Mind, Change Your Physical World."

Deepak Chopra has written many books over the years on the mind-body connection. We are seeing today more evidence that not only can we use our minds to heal depression, chronic fatigue syndrome, weight issues, high blood pressure, and even cancers, we are seeing studies that our physical universe can actually change using the power of the mind. We have the ability to tune in to the subconscious mind, other peoples' minds, and the superconscious mind—or as some have put it, the mind of God, and harvest the power that comes from this infinite source. Since you alone rule your mind, it is up to you to which thoughts you focus on and what the world you live in will look like!

Whenever you ask yourself a question, you are fine-tuning your mind to seek the answer. This is a simplified version of how the mind works. But ask and you will receive the answer. Questions focus the mind. When you change your focus, you will consequently bring in a new awareness. When you change your awareness, you will change what you *know*. When you change what you know, you will have a new understanding. When you change your understanding, many times your feelings will change. When you change your feelings, you will most likely change your actions and ultimately change your destiny. This is the power of asking the right questions. It puts you in charge of a compelling destiny.

Thinking is a process of asking and answering questions. You are constantly engaged in this activity. Psychologists tell us that the average person has about 60,000 thoughts each day. *What most people don't know is that the average person also asks the same questions over and over, resulting in the same 60,000 thoughts the next day.* Is it any wonder why things stay the same? How can things change if you think, say, and do the same things over and over? You must focus your mind in a new direction and change the questions that you are asking for real change to take place.

Your greatest thinking shows up in all areas of your life. What you believe, and the questions you ask, is either propelling you to unending success or stopping you dead in your tracks. Simply put, if you want to change your conditions, then you must change your thinking process. You alone are responsible for your thoughts, and consequently, only you can change them.

So how can you change your thinking? Here is a proven formula for making quantum improvements in your thinking and life: Set a strong intention for what you want, be absolutely honest with yourself, ask an empowering question, gently quiet your mind, patiently listen for the deep answers (which may be either simple or profound), and finally, take the right actions. If you don't get the answer immediately, don't be impatient. Dive deeper and keep asking until the answers come. Remember, when you hear the truth, you will know it. If you have any doubts, it may not be the truth for you. Note: If you are a person who has a habit of doubting, you may not know the truth when you hear it. For you, I suggest paying close attention to your choices, going as far as writing down each choice you make, so you will know when you are tuning in to a worldly thought or your own intuition. As you learn to embrace your intuition, the right actions follow easily.

You can change your thoughts and beliefs almost instantly when you clearly understand your current reality, know what has been stopping your success, have a well-defined vision of where you want to be, possess a strong purpose for getting there, and devise and follow an action plan to achieve your goals.

Let's briefly discuss the mind and how to tap into this treasure chest of resources.

There are three main areas of the mind: the conscious, subconscious, and superconscious. The *conscious* mind is composed of your current perceptions and what you think is real. The *subconscious* mind represents all the thoughts, memories, and emotions that your conscious mind has perceived, interpreted, and recorded over your lifetime, and now lie buried below the level of daily consciousness. You can access your subconscious mind through hypnosis or simple questions designed to awaken this powerful part of your mind. The *superconscious* mind is where true genius, wisdom, power, and joy are located. This is your connection to your source.

Like an iceberg, most of which is hidden beneath the waves, the answers to your deepest questions live in the part of your mind that is mostly beneath your awareness. Remember that the expanse of iceberg beneath the surface is just as real as is the tip above. Similarly, the expanse of the superconscious mind that embraces both your conscious and subconscious mind is just as real. This part of the mind is like a treasure chest, full of jewels and unlimited wealth, just waiting for you to open it.

You can access your superconscious mind by quieting your thoughts and asking powerful questions. Pray to God first, for He is your greatest resource. When the superconscious mind contacts the divine, it is assured of success, because it is attuned with God's unlimited power. Provide your mind with the gift of deep contemplation by being very still. Notice what comes up and practice listening to yourself. Ask anything you want to know and then wait quietly as you observe your thoughts. You need not make any effort. Just sit in silence and observe from the depths of total stillness. As your intuition swings into action, you will clearly hear the answers to your questions. This lucid voice will open up your creativity and allow you to connect to your inner source of truth. You will recognize what you truly believe and what actions you want to take with ease and grace.

The superconscious mind is where your reservoir of life force is located. It is the source of unfathomable wisdom, creativity, and joy. When you learn to draw from the deep well of your mind enthusiastically and deliberately, you will increase and multiply your innate resources until you are saturated with unbounded success and happiness. You will quickly realize what a hopeless task your conscious mind engages in each time you try to manage your affairs without accessing your all-knowing superconscious mind.

The superconscious mind has never been influenced by either your conscious or subconscious mind. It has never known a negative belief, word, or action. It is the living part of your divine inheritance. When you tap into your superconscious mind, every part of your world will change quickly and bring you unending success and joy.

The secret to progress is through self-analysis by daily asking high-minded questions. Introspection is a mirror in which you can sort out where you are strong and what is impeding you. Learn to examine yourself dispassionately. Find out who you *are*, not what you merely fantasize yourself to be! For example, in the evening when you retire, create some time to ask some of the questions in the book that resonate with you. Commit to doing this for a week and see what kind of results show up. For instance, you may ask, "What great memories did I create today? In what areas did I make progress toward my goals? What has to happen for me to create more success in my life? What am I putting up with? What do I keep repeating that is disempowering me? What can I do tomorrow that will change my life for the good"? By doing this, you will become more aware, feel more in control, and ultimately make the changes that are necessary to have an outstanding life.

Focus is the key. Whatever you ask and keep asking, you will find the answer. I repeat: Whatever you ask and keep asking, you will find the answer. This is true for disempowering questions as well as empowering questions. Questions like "Why does this always happen to me?, Why am I such a jerk?, and Why didn't I get the promotion?" will lead you down a path you may not want to go. So, make sure you are asking the *right* questions! The average mind is like a water-soaked matchstick. Scratch it and there is no spark; it will not light. But with the power of asking the right questions with focus, a concentrated mind is like a flare. Strike it and it is immediately aflame with creative ideas flowing outward and upward, which manifest in the material world.

So what has to happen for you to focus your mind and change the way life is showing up for you? First, you must learn the One Question Breakthrough Model. By learning this model, you will tap into the natural way of getting to the right answers for you. These are not someone else's answers. These are the ones that are right for *you*. By consistently following this model, you will see results beyond belief. So, before you answer the questions in the book, commit to the following:

- Never think or say, "I don't know or I can't."
- Be 100 percent honest with yourself.
- Stay with the question until the answer comes.
- Let go of any doubt that you have the answer.
- Take immediate action when the answer arrives.

Now find a place where you will be undistracted. Take a few long, deliberate breaths in while you simultaneously tense the body and then release the tension on the out breath. Next, pick a category in the book where you want to improve. Read through each question in that category and note the ones that you feel compelled to answer. After selecting these questions, read each one, and as you do, reflect upon each word, its meaning, and the meaning of the whole question. Next, close your eyes and allow your honest answer(s) to bubble up to your conscious mind. On the surface, it seems like you may be able to answer most of the questions in the book without much thought. You will be best served, however, by asking the questions many times and then answering the questions after deep contemplation. Sometimes, the answers will not come immediately. It may take days, weeks, or months, but I guarantee that if you stay with the question, and don't turn off the power of the superconscious mind by making statements such as "I don't know, I can't, or I don't care," you will always find the answer that is right for you.

After contemplation, quickly write down your answers in a journal. (It is a good idea to keep a journal of your answers and commitments to review your progress daily.) The *Ask and You Will Succeed Journal* is available online at www.asksucceed.com.

Finally, set a strong intention to make the changes you desire and take immediate action in the direction of that change. Simple, yes! Easy, probably not! It will take focused attention daily to change past habits of thinking and behaving.

You have the power to change. The spirit of inquiry is in all of us. Everyone in this world, sooner or later, will seek success, truth, happiness, and fulfillment. You will seek it either wisely or blindly until you have fully reclaimed yourself. It is never too late to change, improve, or mend. Remember, daily introspection combined with contemplation of the dreams, goals, and desires that burn the hottest in your mind will carry you forward to finding your true power. Just follow your inner compass and it will point the way toward success, freedom, joy, and happiness. Everything is perfectly aligned right now for you to maximize your potential and live the life of your greatest dreams. So never, ever, give up on your dreams. Never give up on having the kind of business you want to have, the kind of relationships you want to have, or the overall quality of life you want to have. Keep asking the right questions and you will succeed!

SECTION 1

Questions for the Big Picture

VALUES CLARIFICATION

Right choice is a function of living our highest values;

so, too, it is the key to a life well lived.

—Kenneth D. Foster

What are values? They are the ideas and principles we hold most highly in our lives. They bring us the most meaning. They're the North Star by which our soul navigates. The values you emphasize in your life may be different from another person's values, but it's surprising that when you ask people about their values, similar themes emerge. There seems to be a spectrum of high values such as justice, courage, love, and dignity that resonate with many people.

In my own life, the values I hold most highly are spiritual values, values of loyalty, values of abundance, family values, and values of friendship. There are two questions you can ask yourself to help you identify your primary values. I've seen people go through long workshops to arrive at understanding how to express their values. But our values are really *already* within each one of us, and if we ask ourselves the right questions, our values will readily reveal themselves.

Ask yourself these questions more than once to get to the core of your values. Your first answer is the surface answer. Subsequent answers will take you deeper. The first question is, "What about success is important to you?" A lot of people will respond, "I don't know." But if you just go to "I don't know," this immediately shuts down your mind. So if you go to "I don't know," ask another question, "If you *did* know, what about success is important to you?"

Someone might say, "It's important to me to take care of my family," "It's important for me to travel and communicate with other cultures," "It's important to me to have God in my life." When you ask yourself the questions, you're just listening for what's valuable. When we define something as *important*, we're on the trail of our values.

The second question I ask is deeper: "What about life is important to you?" This takes a little more thought. It's a good idea to write out what's important to you in life. Then circle the words and phrases that reveal a value to you. You'll eventually come up with what I call your driving values. A driving value is a little different from general values. The driving value is what most motivates your life, and so if you're not living your driving values, you're going to create pain for yourself.

Let's take the example of someone identifying abundance and wealth as being a driving value. If wealth is indeed important to that person, if he chooses a job where the wealth-building capacity is very limited, that's going to create anxiety if wealth is a driving value in the person's psyche. For other people, wealth may not be a driving value. As long as they're getting a paycheck and they're taking care of their needs and their family's needs, that's enough for them. Their driving value might be creativity or the arts, and so they might pursue an artistic career even though it's often challenging to make a lot of money in the arts. Or their driving value might be social activism or counseling and so they pursue the path of working for nonprofit agencies. The important thing is for you to identify what *your own* driving values are.

Another reason to know your values is to help you understand when you're in a value conflict in your relationships. For example, if you really want to have children and you're in a relationship with someone who doesn't want to have children, you've got a major value conflict, particularly if having a child is a driving value in your life. If the two of you end up compromising your values, this doesn't usually work, and sooner or later you will both be consumed by resentment and frustration. It may mean instead that you both have to make choices aligned with your respective highest values, even if this requires that you decide not to be a couple.

If you're not living your values, you will feel stress and discomfort. And that stress and discomfort are *good* because they're the signal that you're alienated from your own values. If you are denying your highest values—your driving values—you're denying yourself. And if you deny yourself long enough, pretty soon you have to map that over with the lies you tell yourself, until you no longer know what is true for you. Sometimes, you just go numb and live your life, as Thoreau put it, in "quiet desperation." Sometimes, you feel exhausted and irritable. Sometimes, you feel that life has lost any sense of fun. Sometimes, you just don't know why you're here. All these are symptoms of lying to yourself about your true values.

If you're in that situation, it's a particularly fortunate moment when you stop in your tracks and say, "How did I get myself into this place of low energy and discontent?" You got yourself there by not living your driving values. The questions of this section will help you get unstuck.

Values are connected to integrity. One huge aspect of integrity is your ability to keep your commitments to yourself. Another equally huge part is being aligned in your thoughts and your actions. Your ability to be in alignment between thought and actions depends on first understanding what your highest values are.

Integrity has a lot to do with telling yourself the truth. Tell yourself the truth about your fears, your strengths, your abilities, your gifts, your shortcomings, what is working in your life, and what is not working. When you do an honest self-evaluation of exactly where you are right now, you're opening yourself up to more integrity coming into your life.

Another thing to consider in pondering values is to know the difference between values and judgment. Very often, we respond to others who hold different values from our own by judging them. While it's true that you want to be in closest relationship with people who share your values, and you make choices in that direction, it's also true that being part of this very diverse society, indeed the global community, will bring you into contact with people whose values you don't share. Sometimes, when we come up against a value conflict, we end up telling ourselves a story about it—we label it and then tell a story. "You should see it this way," or "I don't think that's very responsible; now if I were doing X, I'd do it this way . . ." and so forth.

Being able to separate values from judgment is a mark of spiritual maturity. It's a realization that despite holding different values, we are all *valuable* as human beings. Values are about *you* understanding who you are. It's not about dividing you from everyone else. Let's face it: If everyone held exactly the same values in exactly the same way, life would be very boring. That doesn't mean that you never speak out against injustice. Nor does it mean that you have to accept another's value as being acceptable to you. Again, real spiritual maturity is the ability to speak our own truth and perspective, even if this opposes another, without slipping into judgment of that person as a human being.

Use the questions in this section to help you uncover your own driving values. A really interesting exercise might be to have a friend, colleague, or family member answer the same questions and compare answers. You'll see each other's driving values, and instead of it being a source of conflict or disagreement, it will become a source of dialogue. This may sound idealistic, but if we can't get along with our families, neighbors, coworkers and colleagues, how are we ever going to get along as a nation or as a world citizen? We can use our values to divide us or to promote peaceful dialogue—the choice is up to us.

Values Clarification

Evaluation
> What do you hold dear in life?
> What about success is important to you?
> What about life itself is important to you?
> What do you desire the most in your life?
> What do you love the most in your life?
> What are your five top values?

Vision
> What gives you a sense of freedom?
> What do you want to have?
> What do you want to be?
> What do you want to do?
> If you could have anything in life, what would it be?

Goals
> What specific values will you set a goal around?
> What goals when set by you will change what you value and the
> way you live?

Purpose
> Why is it important to you to live your values?
> When you know your values, what will you know about yourself?
> If you don't live your values, what will that cost you?

Commitment
> Where can you be more courageous in living your values?
> What values are you committed to experiencing on a regular basis?

Blocks to Success
> When do you lie to yourself that you are living a value but you
> really aren't?
> When do you withhold the truth from others?
> Where do you find integrity missing in your life?

Quantum Thinking

Which value could you start living that you are currently not experiencing in your life?

What is the value that, if you chose to live it, would change your life for the better in a very short period of time?

Actions

What five things will you do in the next week to live your top values on a daily basis?

What do you need to say "no" to consistently so that you can actually be in conformance with your highest values?

Support

Who do you know who can support you in living your values?

By what date will you get a support person?

To receive additional information and support, visit Kenneth D. Foster's Living Rich Coaching Community at www.PremierCoaching.com and www.GreatestYearEver.com.

LIFE PURPOSE

Great minds choose a purpose for their lives that inspires

greatness in others.

—Kenneth D. Foster

I began to wake up to my life purpose around 1992 when I sensed a small voice within me saying, "You've got to feel the pain to make the change." I kept hearing these words over and over again in my mind, so I wrote them on a piece of paper and put it on my refrigerator so I could see it until I figured out what it meant.

I was in a lot of pain in my life at the time. I was in a poor relationship. I didn't like my job. I didn't have much of a spiritual life. I had few friendships I could trust. I lived in a city I didn't want to live in. I was alienated from my family. I had gone through a divorce. To put it mildly, I wasn't doing very well. I was in counseling at the time, and when I went in for my weekly session, I asked the counselor what the words that I had heard, "You have got to feel the pain to make the change," meant. The moment he heard the words he paused and looked at me with a long stare. I wasn't expecting what he said next. "Follow the voice. I can't do anything more for you." My several months of counseling with him were over in a flash. As I walked away from the session, I couldn't believe what had just happened and an intense fear for the unknown instantly overtook me as I wondered what I was to do next.

What was this voice the counselor suggested I follow? Did I make it up? Was this real? Well, I decided to find out, so I started listening within my mind to see what else this voice had to say. And to my pleasant surprise it had much to say. The voice led me to a deep self-questioning. It led me to start recovering from the illusions I had created in my life. I was able to see how I had shaped myself as a person whose life wasn't working. I had envisioned myself as a victim of circumstance. I had hallucinated that I was a person "who wasn't good enough or smart enough," a person with no real power—a failure. This inner voice showed me the way out of the pain and how to dispel these illusions of darkness to find the light of truth.

I started to wake up. I began reading. I devoured hundreds of books on spirituality, consciousness, mythology, sociology, success, business—to try to understand the human spirit, *my* spirit. Through it all, I was searching for my life purpose, but it would be awhile before I found it. Or should I say *uncovered* it, for our life purpose has always been with us. We don't always recognize it for what it is, but it is always there.

Some years later, I attended a church service where a facilitator led us through a guided meditation. He had passed out a little white stone to everyone and at the end of the meditation, he asked two questions: "What is your purpose in life and who is your teacher"? I wrote down, "My life purpose is to be an abundant teacher" and on the flip side I wrote the word *Shankara* (which I didn't have any understanding of its meaning until many years later when I began studying Eastern philosophics).

I thought to myself "Abundant teacher? Well, this is a strange life purpose." I wasn't very abundant in my own life at the time. Even though in the past I had run a hundred-million-dollar organization, I had quit that, and I was sitting there, wondering "What am I here to do? What am I here to *be?*" I didn't get immediate answers to these questions. It wasn't "Oh here, this is it!" What I came to understand is that my life purpose was first of all about building an honest foundation of who I am.

So I started to get in touch with what I love to do. I asked: What are my natural skills? What is the soul? How do I connect with my soul? What really matters to me? I created an open mind—what Zen Buddhists call *beginner's mind*—to explore and experience all kinds of possibilities. Through this self-exploration, I learned what was most important to me. I learned what fulfilled me. I learned to overcome blocks, to create possibilities, and to take some of these possibilities from idea to action.

Was this merely a strategy, a set of goals? No, it was the conclusion that my life purpose is to realize my oneness with the divine source of everything. My purpose was to find my way back to that source and then inspire and empower others to do the same. The core of my purpose is love itself—and the discovery of how to express that love in my own life through the lens of my talents, my time, and my treasures of family and friendship. When I turned toward the love within myself, my gifts started flowing forth; my talents revealed themselves. I truly believe that a big part of life's purpose is for you to discover who you really are in your very essence, to find the love and power inside you and to allow it to express itself *through* you in a way that only *you* can.

It's easy to take on someone else's life purpose if you're not careful. Perhaps there is a person in your life who inspires you and you think you want to be like that person. Or perhaps your parents, your spouse, or your peers have formed certain expectations about you. For example, your parents may have said to you, "Your father is a doctor. You're grandfather was a doctor. Your Aunt Mary became a doctor. We come from a long line of doctors. Your calling is to go into medicine." But what if it's not? What if your father's purpose, your grandfather's purpose, and your aunt's purpose is not *your* purpose?

One way to assess whether you're living your own purpose or someone else's is to ask yourself how you feel about where you are in life right now, let's say on a scale of 1 to 10. Is your career a 10? Your relationships? Your leisure time? Your community life? Your spiritual life? This is a good test. If you're feeling unfulfilled in what you're doing, or if you're inspired *some* of the time but *most* of the time you're feeling unfulfilled, that's a good indication you're not following your life's purpose.

This is where self-questioning comes in. The only person who can tell you, beyond all doubt, what your life purpose is, is you. Ask your own heart, and it will answer you. Think of something you feel really drawn to. Ask yourself, "Why is this important to me?" Don't just ask once; ask many times. If you stick with that question, you're going to create an inner passion that connects with your purpose.

Let's say that I ask you, "Why is it important for you to create five thousand dollars a month in your life?"

> "Because I need a good car."
> "Why is that important to you?"
> "Because I'll have the transportation to get my children to school."
> "Why is that important to you?"
> "Because without school, they're not going to succeed in the world."
> "Why is that important to you?"
> "Because I want to do my part to create great human beings who care about the world."

Ahhhhh, life purpose. It's not about the money, or the car, or the school. . . . It's about creating a caring world. Now *that's* something to get passionate about! In my own life, I can say that my life purpose and my service are one and the same. When you follow your purpose, you are offering something very beautiful back to the world. The ultimate purpose, I believe, is to find our way back home to our true self or soul and then to let our light shine in the world. You don't have to be the Dalai Lama or a monk somewhere or a great political leader (unless that is your calling). You simply have to be where you are in the world, where your own gifts can unfold in your own home, your own workplace, your own community. What is your life purpose? Ask your heart, ask your spirit, ask the Divine—then listen and you will hear the answer, the right answer for *you*.

Life Purpose

Evaluation

> What do you believe your life is all about?
>
> What are your greatest talents, skills, and abilities?
>
> What would you be doing in your life if you knew you absolutely could not fail?
>
> If you were just given $10 million, what would be the first thing you would do?
>
> If you learned you had just two years to live, what would you want to accomplish?

Vision

> What is the greatest dream you can imagine accomplishing in your life?
>
> If you could create a perfect life for yourself, what would it look like?
>
> What are your priorities in life?
>
> In what ways does your life purpose align with your vision for your life?

Goals

> What major part of your life would you have to change for you to be more alive and on purpose?
>
> What are three goals you can set for yourself that will support your life purpose?

Purpose

> What causes you to wake up in the morning with enthusiasm?
>
> What turns you on, give you thrills, and makes you feel good inside?

What do you have deep concern or passion for?

What do you know to be your supreme or divine purpose for this life?

What makes you unique?

What things do you daydream about doing?

Commitment

What are you committed to creating no matter what happens?

What would have to happen to increase your level of certainty to complete your life purpose?

Blocks to Success

What do you need to think about differently to have the life you desire?

What could possibly stop you from achieving your life purpose?

Quantum Thinking

What beliefs would a person have to embrace to manifest her life purpose?

If the future of humanity depended on you, what would you do?

What characteristics would you like to be remembered for?

What would you like your epitaph to say?

Actions

What actions will you take to render the greatest possible service?

What is your action plan for fully embracing and fulfilling your life's purpose?

Support

Who do you know who can help you determine your life purpose?

To receive additional information and support, visit Kenneth D. Foster's Living Rich Coaching Community at www.PremierCoaching.com and www.GreatestYearEver.com.

MISSION IN LIFE

Your life cannot be repeated. It is now or never, so find out who you are, what your heart longs to achieve, and then sail away from safe harbors and explore your greatest dreams.

—Kenneth D. Foster

Have you ever wondered what the difference is between your mission in life and your life purpose? Sometimes these words are used interchangeably, but there is a distinction between them. Simply said, your mission encompasses the *actions* you take to enact your purpose. Let's say your life purpose is *to live consciously and courageously, realize the divine within, empower others, and to leave this world a better place.* Your mission may be writing books or teaching classes on business or personal development. Your personal mission, then, is the way you choose to *express* your life purpose. It is the driving action that brings forth your life purpose.

As you live out your life purpose, it may involve many different missions in your lifetime. Usually, when a person feels really strongly about accomplishing something, it's not uncommon to hear that person say, "I'm on a mission to get this done." The key to knowing what your mission (action plan) will be at this point in your life again comes back to self-questioning. Ask yourself, "What do I hope to accomplish right now that will help me realize my life purpose? How do I plan to accomplish my life purpose? What are three goals I can identify as being missions that support my purpose? What are five action steps I can take to realize my life purpose?

I encourage you to answer these questions and then write out your current mission in life. Reflect on how it's connected with your purpose. Then find three people to evaluate your mission statement and see if they believe that this is aligned with what you're really about. This is a powerful step. I was having some financial challenges a few years back. I knew there was a reason that money stopped flowing into my life, but I wasn't seeing it, so I asked a few close friends if they thought what I was doing was aligned with my life purpose. To my surprise, they all said no. This caused me to look again at my life purpose and evaluate if what I was doing was aligned. What I found out was the mission I was on was a mission I had outgrown and had no passion for doing any more. I then chose a new mission and guess what?: the money started flowing in again. Make sure you have some excitement or passion around the mission you choose. When you get clear on how your mission fits your purpose, you'll make better decisions as to what your plan of action is and the values behind your actions. So if your life isn't showing up the way you want, look at your purpose and mission to make sure they are aligned.

Perhaps you have come up with a number of paths that seem to support your purpose. Let's say you want to own a car dealership, you want to start an Internet-based business, and you also want to start a health-related business—all of these possibilities may interest you and may align, to a degree, with a purpose you might have about helping others enhance their lives.

Take some time to reflect on which of the possibilities feels closest to you right now. You might then decide to focus on the health-related business because there is a great need for good health information and products. You might decide on a car dealership so that you can promote fuel-efficient vehicles such as hybrid cars to help preserve the environment. The point is that *you* decide intuitively which mission feels best to you, and then go for it!

You may ask how will I know if it is my intuition or something else. If your mission has aroused a passion and energy within you, it is most likely your intuition speaking to you. Also, if it's your intuition speaking, it's likely that when you express it to others, they will easily get it because they will feel your enthusiasm behind your words. When you tell them your mission, they say "Oh, yes." They'll *get* what you do.

And even more important, *you'll* get what you do! One more thing—don't make your mission too small. Sometimes, the most creative thing we can do, the thing that makes us stretch and grow, is that we put ourselves on what seems to be a Mission Impossible. Know that if your heart really wants to manifest a quality or situation in your life, there is *nothing* that is impossible. When you're on the right mission for *you*, you'll feel the alignment between your knowledge and your feelings. You'll feel organically, with all the intuition inside you, that your mission is congruent with your life purpose. And when the two of these are in harmony, there is no stopping you!

Mission in Life

Evaluation
>What are the 10 greatest lessons that you have learned in your life?
>What gifts do you bring to the world?
>What are your strongest qualities?

What do you want to be remembered for?

What do you want that you have not already achieved?

Vision

If your personal mission were easily visible, what would it look like?

What special work do you see yourself completing?

If you knew in two years you would leave the planet, what would you change?

What have you envisioned for your life?

Goals

What do you want to get out of life?

What has to happen for you to live your mission?

Purpose

What do you stand for?

What is the number one goal in your life?

Why is it important for you to have a mission?

Commitment

What are you committed to doing in this world?

What positive contributions do you make through your work?

Blocks to Success

What do you think could stop you from accomplishing your life's work?

Quantum Thinking

What would your life look like if you accepted the greatest good for yourself daily?

What is the most valuable lesson you have learned in your life so far?

When do you feel most powerful and why?

If there were a secret passion in your life, something almost too exciting to actually do, what would it be?

Actions

What kind of life will you design for yourself?

In what ways can you use what you have learned to enhance the
lives of others?

What are five action steps you can take immediately to create
your mission?

Support

Whom can you talk with to help you clarify your mission in life?

What connections can you make with people who have a mission
similar to yours?

To receive additional information and support, visit Kenneth D. Foster's
Living Rich Coaching Community at www.PremierCoaching.com and
www.GreatestYearEver.com.

SPIRITUAL

In the garden of your heart, find the Master of the universe,
for He will help you water your dreams with love, your
challenges with fearlessness, and your activities with joy.

Kenneth D. Foster

What is it to be spiritual? It's finding our way back home, tapping into our soul and remembering who we are. It's about connecting with a Source that is right within us and realizing our true nature. When we find pain, suffering, or challenges in our life, that is often a call for us to go within and begin to ask ourselves new questions. Questions like "Why am I here on this planet at this time?" or "Who am I at the deepest part of my core?" or "What is the meaning of life?" These questions will lead to answers that can be found only with deep searching because they are found only within our souls.

There have been great leaders in the world, such as Abraham Lincoln, George Washington, and Napoleon Bonaparte, but their victories were only temporary. Many of the issues they dealt with—slavery, democracy, rules of warfare—keep coming around again. It's as if history gives us repeated lessons, not to punish us, but to help us cultivate the consciousness of Spirit. This is why we were born—so that we will exercise our divine powers to find God.

There have been great devices given to us by science to make our lives easier, but their help, too, is only temporary. Our cars break down, the latest computer lasts for only a few years, and so on. *External things only bring temporary happiness*. Most people are on an eternal quest to find that Something that will make them happy. The real happiness, though, comes from mastering yourself and finding God. For those who have used their minds, will, and actions to ask the deeper questions—who have sought and found God—the search is over. They have found the Something.

The development of our intuition is one of the keys to creating a successful life. Did you know that your intuition is right 100 percent of the time? So, what has to happen for you to learn how to use and trust your intuition? Most errors in intuition come about not because of the intuition itself but because of our propensity to doubt the message we're getting from our inner self. Wouldn't you like to make better choices in life? Wouldn't you like to have more wisdom in your life? If so, the development of your intuition is the key. Using your intuition helps you learn to look at your life from a *spiritual* point of view rather than from a worldly point of view.

To live a spiritual life, you must learn to apply spiritual principles in your daily life. Let's take the principle of Calmness, or what some traditions call *equanimity*. The goal in this example will be to maintain a neutral mind—which results in calmness—in every changing condition. The first step is to set a strong intention to stay calm. Then ask an enlightened question, something like "What thoughts can I hold in my mind to stay calm in all situations today?" You will get several answers, such as "I am loved" or "I am filled with a calm spirit" or "I know I am filled with the peace of God." Then, hold your answers in your mind throughout the day. You may want to write them down, so that if you are tempted to get caught up in some drama, you will remember to keep your thoughts attuned to the goal of staying calm. The answers you get when you ask enlightened questions come from higher realms of your consciousness. It is beyond the common thoughts of the conscious or subconscious mind.

A good way to test your spiritual progression is to begin right at home with your family! For many years, as I visited my family, I could tell how far I had come along, or how much I needed to work on myself, by how I reacted to the drama in my home life. And let's face it: everyone's family dynamics has drama! For example, I watched myself when my dad would say something that I didn't agree with. Would I get angry and defend myself by reacting with a negative comment, or would I stay neutral, connected to my center, and let it be? When he would react to circumstances in his environment, would I commiserate with him or give him compassion about what he was going through?

Most people think they need to take on the circumstances of life. They feel defeated by circumstances. Circumstances in our life, though, are the tests that bring out either the best in us or the worst. Either way, we have the opportunity to learn, grow, change, and improve. Whether the challenges we face are in the area of our health, in our relationships, or in our work environment, they are here for one purpose: to help us dive deep within ourselves, to the consciousness of our spirit, and to bring out the Divine within us.

We have to go within and find the divine consciousness that lies within our soul to be able to live an authentically full life. If we just stay focused on the surface of our lives or the outer consciousness, not much changes. The people in our lives may change or the job may change or where you live may change, but there will not be significant changes on the inside. That's why, without consciousness of our patterns and our connection to spirit, many of us keep repeating the same patterns over and over again. In fact, I have known many people who hold on to the same beliefs year after year and have the same problems year after year.

As a spiritual being, you can learn to use your mind for psychological victory over yourself—for self-mastery. You can do this by analyzing where you have failed and where you have succeeded. You look at what's working in your life and what's not working. Then ask the right questions around what has to happen to change what is not working, and focus more of our attention and energy on what *is* working.

The ultimate discovery on the spiritual path is God realization. And because we can't navigate through this universe completely alone, it's important to call on the Divine to assist us. You have heard the saying, "Let go and let God." I say, "Let go and *ask* God!" Truly find out how you can realize God in each moment of your life. One very effective way of doing this is through the power of questioning.

One of the biggest things I have learned is that life is difficult and filled with a lot of adversity and challenges, but those challenges aren't in fact bad. They are part of the blessing life has given me—an opportunity to grow as a human being. I used to spend all my time avoiding anything that was hard, finding shortcuts for everything possible—work, family, friends, emotions, relationships, and so on. As a result of avoiding those pieces of life, I never grew as a person. But now I know when challenging circumstances and problems show up, we find the source of our power. It is that power that will destroy all darkness in our lives. It is when we learn to tap into the spiritual power that lies within each of us that we transcend all troubles.

I have found over the years that it is important to set spiritual goals. Most people I speak with have never taken the time to do this. They have personal goals or goals for their businesses but never set goals to take them closer to God. I would suggest you break down your spiritual life into four categories—Meditation, Prayer, Service, and Contribution—and set goals in each area. For example, you could set a goal to meditate morning and evening for the next year or learn to pray deeply from your heart, with earnestness. Or you could commit to serving at your temple or church, or set a goal to contribute 10 percent more each month than you did last year.

If you will include spiritual goals in your life, you will be amazed at how much more fulfilled you become and how much more good you can bring into this world.

Take some time now to ask yourself the questions that follow. Allow yourself quiet, uninterrupted time to go within. And then, take immediate action on a daily basis to help you tap into the beautiful, spiritual side of yourself. Blessings to you on your journey!

Spiritual

Evaluation
What is your quest in life?
What insights do you have about why you were created?
What have you always known to be true in your life?
What do you know about your Soul?

Vision
What do you yearn for in the deepest part of your Soul?
What is the essence of your being?
What do you want to proclaim to the universe?
What is your highest vision of God?

Goals
What are your goals for connecting with God?
Why were you born on this planet and what will you accomplish?
What has to happen for you to consciously connect with your
    Soul on a daily basis?
What goals can you set to feel a deeper love for your Creator?

Purpose
What were you born to do?
Who are you becoming?
Why is it important for you to realize the essence of you?

Commitment
What are the three most powerful spiritual principles you are
    committed to learning?

Blocks to Success
>Where have you limited the unlimited?
>Is there anything that seems to lessen your feeling of God?

Quantum Thinking
>What is God's dream for your life?
>What is the greatest lesson death can teach you?
>What have you learned about the other side?
>What beliefs have to shift in you so that you know there are no limits to what you can accomplish with your life?
>If you could devise the best strategy for your spiritual evolution, what would it be?
>What would you like God to say to you?

Actions
>What can you do to deepen your experience of God?
>What five ways can you increase your faith?
>What can you do for God today?

Support
>Who is a realized teacher, preacher, guru, or sage that can support you in experiencing God in your life?
>Who knows God and would be willing to mentor you to find God?

To receive additional information and support, visit Kenneth D. Foster's Living Rich Coaching Community at www.PremierCoaching.com and www.GreatestYearEver.com.

CONTRIBUTION

Service is the way we say thanks for all that has been given to us.

—Kenneth D. Foster

When you turn on the evening news, what do you usually see? Murders, robberies, financial scandals, wars, children suffering, economic woes . . . all appearing to be harbingers of the apparent downfall of society. A common reaction to this is often the sense of hopelessness or defeat. You feel powerless. You say to yourself, "There is nothing much I can do to help the world. The problems are just too huge." And you feel even more disheartened.

The media focus on these events to grab your attention. After all, dramatic tension-filled stories make for great news copy! If you let your attention be influenced by all of this global negativity, you can inadvertently end up becoming part of the problem rather than part of the solution.

The eighteenth-century philosopher Edmund Burke once said, "All that is necessary for the triumph of evil is that good men do nothing" (excuse Burke's gendered language; today we would rephrase that as "when good people do nothing"). The media, by focusing daily on hundreds, if not thousands, of negative images almost ensure that many good people, simply from feeling overwhelmed, will indeed do nothing.

But here is the real scoop: There are all kinds of amazing and wonderful things happening around the world. We just don't hear about them as news. There are generous people everywhere giving their hearts, their time, their money, and their love to help just the right people in the right place when they need it most.

What you focus on expands. So, if you focus your attention on the negativity out there, there is a good chance you will internalize those thoughts inside you and expand that negativity into your life by commenting on what you have seen with others. The quantum scientists tell us, "Thoughts become things." That everything is energy and energy affects energy. So, a great place to start contributing in life is to be a positive force for good.

When you find yourself having thoughts that are less than positive, notice them, and stop them from growing. Ask yourself, "Have I given my power away to a person, circumstance, or thing?" If so, remind yourself that you have the power to control your thinking and that there are solutions to almost everything. Beauty is all around us . . . *if* we choose to see it. The more we feel helpless and that we don't have much of an impact in the world, the more that becomes our story. On the flip side, the more we step out of our box and decide each day who we will be, and how we will affect the lives of others . . . wonderful opportunities will magically present themselves.

To live a fulfilling life, we've got to genuinely feel appreciation for who we are and what we have, and then pay it forward by giving to others. How did you feel the last time you stopped at a lemonade stand and presented a few quarters to the neighborhood child who so patiently monitored her stand on the corner? Or how about when you let someone who was in a hurry at the grocery store go ahead of you in line? It feels *good* to give to others . . . even in these small ways. I love to do things for others and not let them know it was me. I get to see their joy and can remain anonymous.

You've probably heard the phrase about how it's "better to give than to receive." There's a reason why this little phrase has hung around for so long. Because not only does it feel good when you give, but every person I know who tithes on a regular basis is living an abundant life. In fact, they life a much different life from people who don't give on a regular basis! Giving also helps us feel more purposeful, like there is direction to our lives, rather than just floating along. And once we become locked in to living *on purpose*, life is good!

I was working with Anthony Robbins a few years ago. My team was flown into Atlanta, Georgia, for an event. One evening, my team went to dinner at a local Waffle House Restaurant. We were waited on by a young waitress who was a single mother with a five-year-old daughter. I asked the waitress a few questions and found out she was struggling financially, so our team decided to leave her a tip that would blow her away. When the meal was finished and the bill for $39.00 came, we decided to leave a one-hundred-dollar tip. We placed the tip under the bill so she wouldn't see it immediately. We then all left the restaurant and walked outside.

The table we had been sitting at was right in front of a large glass window, and because it was dark outside we could see in, but the waitress could not see out. We watched as she went to pick up our bill and tip. When she saw the tip, she actually jumped in the air for joy, and when she landed, she had a huge smile with tears coming down her face. We watched as she ran over to another waitress and told her the news of her one-hundred-dollar tip, all the while waving the bill in her hand and jumping up and down. As we all watched her reaction, we felt a deep sense of connection to her and we also had tears in our eyes. Yes, giving really brings us joy!

If you would like to get in touch with how to contribute before you leave the planet, then imagine yourself at the end of your life and ask a few simple questions. Have you found joy in your life? What will your life have been about? Who has become better off because you were here? Where have you made a difference? When you can really step into and visualize this place—the end of your life, looking back—then you can tap into how you truly would like to make a difference.

You have the power to change this world for the better. It is right inside of you, just waiting for you to ask some new questions and make a wise choice. So, take some time today and choose where and to whom you will contribute. The songwriter Jana Stanfield wrote a song lyric with the words "I cannot do all the good the world needs, but the world needs all the good I can do." That's an admirable motto to live by. Don't focus on all the things you can't do; ask instead, "What *can* I do to make a difference today? The people whose lives you desire to touch are waiting for you. They *need* you. Our lives are like a spider web, intricately woven, and whatever path we choose affects the rest of the world.

Now give yourself the gift of going inward. Take some time to explore the questions that follow and find out who it is that you really desire to be in the world. Then, decide how you can pool your resources, your gifts, and your passions to make this world a better place. The rest of us graciously thank you in advance!

Contribution

Evaluation

What is your most treasured memory of how you have contributed to society?

What is the most significant understanding or insight you have gained from society?

What are the greatest ways you will benefit humanity?

Where is your greatest desire to serve?

In what areas do you make a difference in the world?

To this point in your life, what has been your greatest contribution to society?

Vision

What new memories would you like to create while contributing to society?
What trend or trends in society would you like to change?
What is your greatest vision of your contribution to the world?
What could you say yes to that would change society for the better?
What aspect of society troubles you the most and what will you do about it?

Goals

What are your top goals for your contribution to society?
What would have to happen to make your goals twice as large?

Purpose

Why do you want to create change in the world?
What do you feel when you make a real difference to others?
What areas are you deeply called to contribute?

Commitment

What commitment will you make and keep to make a huge difference in the world?

Blocks to Success

What are you saying no to that keeps society the way it is?
What is keeping you from contributing to society in a big way?

Quantum Thinking

If you had the ability to change the world instantly, what would you change?
In what areas can you dare to be different?
What service can you provide that will positively affect thousands of people?
In what ways can you bring greater joy into the world through your contributions?

Actions

What actions will you take this week to make a difference in the world?

Support

Who is your greatest philanthropic role model who can mentor you?

Whom could you team up with to increase the impact of your contributions and theirs?

To receive additional information and support, visit Kenneth D. Foster's Living Rich Coaching Community at www.PremierCoaching.com and www.GreatestYearEver.com.

SECTION 2

Questions to Grow Your Potential

BELIEFS

When a man stops thinking in limited terms,

he starts knowing unlimited success.

—Kenneth D. Foster

Our beliefs *about* ourselves form the basis of our belief *in* ourselves. When you believe in yourself, you are capable of limitless achievement. Your accomplishments, in turn, confirm your belief in yourself, and you create an upward spiral of positive thought and action. Even if you might stumble along this course, as we all do at some time in our lives, you can always change your beliefs and return to that upward spiral.

Strong beliefs or convictions are built by making commitments to yourself and making good on those commitments. You keep these promises by engaging in positive self-talk and self-affirmations that motivate and guide you toward your goals. By the same token, you need to flip the script on your negative messages to yourself. You can and must take responsibility for your thoughts—transform them—just as you take responsibility for your actions. There is *will*-power, and there is *won't*-power.

The best way to start redirecting your thought process is to ask yourself questions. Not just any questions, but the positive-focused and enlightened questions that are listed in each chapter throughout this book.

Positive questions go like this: What are my strengths? What am I good at? What do I love about myself? The answers are as varied as grains of sand on the beach: I am honest. I am trustworthy. I've got a beautiful golf swing. I'm a wizard when it comes to surfing the net. I'm a great karaoke singer. I'm an effective communicator. I'm a good listener. I have a beautiful smile.

In my coaching practice, I ask clients to come up with 10 positive attributes daily for 10 days. Then I ask them to narrow that down to their 20 most important positive qualities, then the five things they most admire about themselves. I have them memorize these five affirmations and practice saying them to themselves. This is the essence of positive self-talk and of developing new, productive-thinking habits and beliefs.

Then the next step would be the enlightened questions: Who am I? What is my purpose on Earth? What is the nature of boundless abundance? There are no easy answers to enlightened questions. They must be contemplated on the deepest level, approached with imagination and unflinching self-analysis. These questions help you to understand what makes you tick. The more aware we are of the realities of our lives, the more empowered we are to produce change.

The affirmations that arise from positive questions, and the reflection that is born of enlightened questions, combine to raise self-awareness and stimulate belief in oneself. What most people find, however, is that they've never asked themselves these questions! They've never learned to locate worthiness within themselves. They rely on acknowledgment from others for their sense of worth. To keep this external assignment of value coming, they tend to give more of themselves to others than is emotionally, and sometimes physically, healthy.

I once had a client in the medical profession come to me for help in straightening out her finances. Each of her patients was allotted a set amount of her time. But, as I soon discovered, she increasingly found herself going over the time limit. She quickly fell behind schedule and became overwhelmed by the demands on her time. The fact is that she sought acknowledgment from her patients. On an unconscious level, she believed she would lose that approval if she ended the session before the patient seemed ready.

During my work with this client, I also learned that she loved to shop. While at a coaching session in her home, I saw that the place was festooned with stuff—piles of books and CDs, exercise equipment, clothes, and shoes still in shopping bags, an abundance of furniture and knickknacks, toys for her two dogs. It became clear that her self-worth was determined not only by the people in her life, but by the *things* in her life.

Through positive self-talk, she began to redirect her beliefs about herself. Then we introduced some leverage to help her break what had become a very bad habit. We decided that whenever she let a client go beyond his allotted appointment time, she would have to give $100 to the charity of her choice. That way, if she lost, at least *someone* would win. This combination of the carrot (self-affirmations and enlightened understanding) and the stick (donations to charity) was effective. We'd gotten to the crux of the issue, and at its core, the problem was one of faulty beliefs, resting on external sources.

Once we uncovered that piece of the puzzle, things started to open up. She began to find worth in herself. Positive thought led to positive action, which ultimately led to positive results. She began establishing boundaries and respecting them. She was more fulfilled at work, from which her patients and colleagues benefited enormously. She started to publish in her field and develop a national reputation. In short, she manifested her destiny.

For this client, something clicked. For others, the process is like the peeling of an onion. It may proceed very gradually. It may not follow a linear path. We're not perfect. People have setbacks. I have seen firsthand the upset of negative thoughts, how they breed fear, anger, judgment, contempt, hopelessness. They cause emotional paralysis. And they block the realization of potential. Enlightened thoughts, on the other hand, tap into the super-conscious mind of life. They help us locate and access our genius. They instill in us a profound sense of well-being. They foster creativity, confidence, and love. They nurture the flower of our selves.

When you change your thoughts, and by virtue of this, your actions, your world starts to shake. You feel the reverberations of your determination in every aspect of your being. Your spirit is awakened. Small things—the way you dress, the way you carry yourself—are altered. Your home life becomes more harmonious. Your relationships deepen to a level previously unima-gined. And the people in your life respond. They amend their own thoughts and actions. They are carried with you along the upward spiral.

Spend some time now examining your own beliefs. Get real with yourself and see what you find. The questions that follow will help you identify beliefs that support your growth and development, as well as uncover old, unhealthy beliefs that are repeatedly blocking your path to success.

The ability to activate the positive thought-and-action chain is within the power of each and every one of us. Belief is ours. We *can* make the changes that lead to the lives we truly want to live. As I like to tell my clients, "It's all an inside job."

Beliefs

Evaluation

Up to now, what kind of life have you created with your current beliefs?

What kind of thoughts do you dwell upon the most?

What old habits of thinking and action are no longer serving
   you?
What thoughts strengthen you and what thoughts weaken you?
What do you want to improve with regard to your thinking?
What questions do you consistently ask yourself?
What do you truly believe about yourself?

Vision

What would you truly like to change or improve upon?
What habits would you like to change?
What circumstances would you like to change?
What relationships would you like to change?
Where would you like to develop, improve, and grow?

Goals

What are your top three priorities when it comes to changing
   your thinking?
What are two habits you will be letting go of?

Purpose

What are your five top reasons to develop new empowering
   beliefs?
Why is it important for you to master your mind?

Commitment

What new habits are you committed to developing?

Blocks to Success

Where are you critically judging yourself?
What is the cause of you making poor choices?
What do you believe is keeping you stuck?
In the past, what has stopped you from breaking negative habits?

Quantum Thinking

If you were to take full responsibility for your beliefs, what might
   your new life look like?
What new beliefs will let you move past difficulties forever?
What do you believe must change for you to have more success?

Actions

What actions can you take to avoid pain and gain more pleasure and happiness?

What three things could you do each week to help you develop empowering beliefs?

Support

Who can support you in forming new empowering beliefs?

What three books will really support you in mastering your mind?

Who do you know who can mentor you to use your mind in a very productive way?

To receive additional information and support, visit Kenneth D. Foster's Living Rich Coaching Community at www.PremierCoaching.com and www.GreatestYearEver.com.

PERSONAL DEVELOPMENT

*Personal growth starts with your thoughts, for no
one experiences anything that they don't hold first
in their mind.*

—Kenneth D. Foster

The journey of personal development oftentimes begins when stress, anxiety, deep hurt, or pain is felt. When there are no real answers coming from friends, therapists, counselors, or mentors, it is time to delve within and ask some very deep questions. Questions like, "Why am I getting the results I am getting in my life and what can I do to create change?" Or "If I don't make changes now, what will my life be like in three years?" Or "What is the real purpose of my life?" This is the best time to identify what you are putting up with and what is your part in creating this. It is a time to become very honest with yourself and assess all areas of your life, including: home, work, spiritual, leisure time, relationships, financial, and health.

Personal development is another name for Personal Empowerment and never have the opportunities for help with personal development been greater than today! In the past decade, the personal development industry has exploded. There are books, speakers, coaching programs, teleclasses— all kinds of venues and formats to choose from. The advantage of this unprecedented growth is that almost everyone can find a book, a program, a coach, or an idea or approach they can resonate with.

Even though there is indeed an information-rich universe out there that can provide you with ample opportunities for learning, inner self-questioning still remains the most effective route of personal development.

Simply beginning the process of inquiry and looking within starts the process of personal development, which ultimately leads to a more successful life. Personal development opens us up to the possibilities of who we are and what our gifts and talents are.

We begin to explore what we can accomplish. When we start going within, we begin to tap deep into the recesses of our unrealized potential. We begin to understand our life purpose and realize what we have to contribute to the world. We begin to understand that life is best lived when we have support around us.

This is where the mentors and coaches come in. Coaches and mentors are not meant to be the replacement for our self-questioning; they're meant to enhance it. And as we tap into our own innate wisdom, we begin to become conscious of and receive the guidance from our own Higher Self, or as some might say, the consciousness of the Divine.

When we look underneath the surface level of the mind we will find the gifts, beliefs, experiences, and talents that helped us get where we are and also the unhealthy habits or patterns of behavior that keep us stuck, running in circles, and elude us from realizing our full potential.

Most of my clients come to me because they want to grow, improve, or change. And many of them want to know what they needed to do to be happier, more productive, and feel a deeper sense of fulfillment in their lives. They want me to help them see the patterns in their lives that were out of balance, so they could make the necessary changes. I noticed that some were successful in their careers and yet their finances were a mess. Or they were successful in their social lives but their relationships were in turmoil. Or their careers were blossoming, but their health was out of balance.

I found that many people had some sort of disconnect between the different areas of their lives. Everything counts, though, and what is showing up in one area of their life is generally affecting and is connected to other areas of their life, whether they're aware of it or not. Think about your life for a moment and ask yourself, "What am I not aware of that is affecting my life?" Or, pick an area of your life that is not working and ask yourself, "How is this area of my life (like having little money or a disconnected relationship) affecting all the other areas of my life?" When you ask these types of questions, you have started the personal development process and if you stay in the question until you get the answer and then commit to making changes, your life will soon improve.

Personal development starts to break down the disempowering choices and patterns of thought that stop us from experiencing true joy and peace in all areas. To know if this is the right time for personal development in your life, you might ask:

1. Do I experience joy on an ongoing basis?
2. Am I contributing joy to others?
3. Do I have a sense of fulfillment in all areas of my life?
4. Have I realized a deep sense of personal wisdom in my life?
5. Am I at peace with myself?

If the answer is no to any of these questions, then it is very clear that it's time to turn the light of introspection on the areas of your life that are challenging.

The end result of personal development is truly amazing and rewarding. You begin to develop your intuition, which leads to greater wisdom, which leads to better choices, which leads to increased success, which ultimately leads to exponential happiness and joy!

There is only one word of caution in all this—don't allow personal development programs to overrun your life. Don't let them become an excuse to keep you away from your own inner wisdom through self-questioning and reflection. I have had a few clients over the years who defined themselves and were proud to be labeled "Personal Development Junkies." They chased every new book and every new personal development guru that came on the scene. The result was that even though they thought they were growing, many years would pass and there was no real change for them. Their finances were the same; their relationships were the same; their living conditions were the same; in fact, in all areas of life that they defined as relevant to them, there was no real change. They had fallen into the great personal development illusion of turning your thinking and power over to another who gives you his wisdom and advice on how you should live your life.

There is only one way out from this illusion. They had to become very honest with themselves and look at the results that they were getting in their life. This was painful for most of them, but as I pointed out to them, the truth is more powerful than illusions, and when they started on a program of meditation and deep introspection to find their own answers, life started getting better quickly for most.

Personal development work can and does lead to quickened self-growth, but it is imperative not to turn your power over to someone who thinks she knows how to run your life better than you do. Your answers will come in the long run from developing your own intuition, will, reason, and focused actions.

Over the many years of coaching, I have not run across anyone who didn't have many great gifts and talents. Everyone has genius within them and has the power to change his life for the better. Find what works for you and what doesn't. Then incorporate the new principles you learned into your life and apply them. Above all, be sure to follow up whatever you're doing in the area of personal development by asking yourself the important questions in this section. Powerful questions are the greatest personal development of all! Ask and you will succeed.

Personal Development

Evaluation

What does your thinking look like to others?
What is the greatest regret of your life?
What have been your biggest challenges through life?
What have you learned from your greatest mistakes?
What parts of yourself are difficult to accept?
In what areas have you let yourself down?
What is great about your past?
Where have you limited your power?

Vision

What is your greatest response to the challenges of everyday life?
What is the greatest vision you have for your life?
In what areas do you see yourself developing more faith and
    courage?
What brings you the greatest joy?
What do you anticipate will be great about your future?

Goals

What is your plan for personal development?
What are your goals, dreams, hopes, and aspirations?

Purpose

What are you really after in life?
What are you capable of accomplishing in your life?
Why is personal development important to you?
What will determine the quality of your life?

Commitment

What are you willing to take ownership of in your quest for
    personal growth?
In what areas of your life are you committed to becoming more
    competent?
What are you committed to learning that will accelerate your
    personal growth?
What are you committed to doing that will eliminate your
    struggle forever?
What are you committed to starting or stopping?

Blocks to Success

Which of your personal traits would you like to change the most?

What don't you want others to know about you?

What bad habits do you want to transform into good habits?

What have you been wishing and hoping for rather than going all-out for?

What do you fear the most and how is that fear affecting your life?

What voids in your life are you trying to fill?

What do you need to release to permanently free yourself from guilt and shame?

Quantum Thinking

What is the most profound way that failure has helped you gain an edge in life?

Imagine you have the ability to see the world with different eyes—the eyes of a spiritual person, or a wealthy person or a joyful person—what would your world look like?

What can you accept today that will change all your tomorrows?

What do you need to feel great every day?

Actions

What is the best way for you to get started on a path of personal growth?

What could you do in the next two weeks to face and release your fears?

What actions can you take to turn your difficulties into extraordinary opportunities?

Support

Where does your power come from?

Whom can you identify as a possible mentor for your personal development?

Where can you find a mentor or a coach to support your personal transformation?

To receive additional information and support, visit Kenneth D. Foster's Living Rich Coaching Community at www.PremierCoaching.com and www.GreatestYearEver.com.

BOUNDARIES

*Success is determined by a person's character, and
character is determined by the promises you keep to
yourself and others.*
—Kenneth D. Foster

Imagine you have been working very hard, putting in many hours on a project you've just completed. You promised yourself that when the project was finished, you would take some time to rejuvenate and reconnect with your spirit. Well, tonight is the night! You've done the job. You have set up a massage for yourself, then dinner at your favorite restaurant and a walk around a nearby serene lake.

Ahhh . . . a much-needed evening of self-care! But then, a surprise phone call comes to you from the president of an organization where you volunteer. A call for help; they need you to pitch in tonight. You can't believe you took the call and that the president asked you, when there were so many others available to help. So your typical knee-jerk reaction kicks in and you put on your happy face for the president and say, "Sure."

But then you hang up the phone feeling discouraged, disappointed, and less than enthusiastic about your role as volunteer. You realize that you have made a poor choice and have sabotaged your most important commitment—the commitment to nurture and take care of yourself. You have been longing for the massage, dinner, and walk respite you had scheduled for yourself, as it would be time for you to slow down, reflect, and just be. You knew it was important to you; you simply made the wrong decision. Instead of being true to yourself and nurturing your spirit, you decided to please another.

Can you relate? Has this ever happened to you? If so, do you know why? Well, first let me tell you it has nothing to do with being weak-willed or not strong enough to stand up to others' requests. There are many times when we all make good choices that support our values and commitments to ourselves. But in those times that we don't stand up for ourselves, what can we do differently?

It is simple; we can ask questions that will empower us, like "What is the boundary I must set for myself to live a balanced life?" No one will ever set a boundary for you. It is up to you to empower yourself or disempower yourself!

When you have broken a commitment to yourself, take that time to reflect on how you could do things differently. Questions like: "What am I committed to having in my life?" or "What has to happen for me to set clear boundaries?" will get you the right answers. When I first started my coaching business, I accepted clients at basically any time, day or night. I wanted to fill my practice up. I had 21 clients in my first month, and just as I had visualized it, the sessions were day and night. I had no time for myself. I allowed clients to go way over their coaching time. I never said no.

Whenever they called, I picked up the phone. I was trying to create a successful practice, but I ended up creating a situation in which I was feeling drained, overwhelmed, and running on empty. It soon became clear to me that I needed to set some boundaries. And so I did. I decided that I would coach only on Tuesday, Wednesday, and Thursday. The times for coaching would be between 9:00 and 5:00. I decided to value my services more, so I charged more for my time. I would let clients know 10 minutes before their time was up that we would be wrapping up. I charged extra fees for clients who showed up late or who went overtime. And I was astounded to find that it all worked out just fine—the clients readily accepted my new conditions. When I chose to set a boundary for myself and made it clear, they chose to respect it—funny how that works!

Remember that in each moment you have a choice. You can choose to honor your boundaries or not. And in each moment of choice (for example, an unexpected invitation to volunteer), you can pause before answering. You pause to check in about your boundary; pause to make sure it is being honored.

Ask yourself a simple question: "What boundary am I committed to and how will I feel if I break it?" Then, after reflecting on your boundary or commitment, you're ready to make your decision.

To replay the volunteer scenario from a different perspective, the phone call comes in and you are asked to volunteer. This time, you take a brief moment to ask, "What boundary am I committed to and how will I feel if I break it?" Then you remember! "Tonight is a special gift to myself and I deserve to have some quiet time alone, and the important volunteer role could surely be filled by someone else that night. I would feel disempowered if I break my commitment to myself." Then you answer: "Thanks so much for asking . . . I appreciate you thinking of me. I'm sorry, but I'm not able to work tonight. I hope it's not too hard to find someone else." All said with a smile because you *know* what is best for you.

You have created a healthy boundary. You know that when you go to bed later that night, you will feel refreshed, invigorated . . . and above all, true to yourself.

Healthy boundaries start with honoring ourselves and acknowledging the current reality of what is needed in the moment. Wouldn't you agree that self-care is a priority? If so, then, look at the questions in this section and pick out the ones that will direct your mind into getting the right answers for you to set up healthy boundaries in all areas of your life.

Boundaries

Evaluation
> Where are people taking advantage of you?
> What areas of your life seem out of control?
> Where do you give too much?
> Where do you feel your energy is being drained?
> What is your most effective boundary?
> Where have boundaries served you?

Vision
> What is the meaning of healthy boundaries to you?
> Imagine a life that is on purpose, organized, and time managed well. What will that look like for you?
> In what areas will you benefit by putting effective boundaries in place?
> When do you need to say no more often?
> In which areas of your life would you like to have better boundaries?

Goals
> What is the first area of your life that a strong boundary will help you get back control of your life?
> What are three goals you can set and accomplish with regard to having healthy boundaries?

Purpose
> Why is it important to you to have healthy boundaries?

What will it mean to you and your family when you have non-negotiable boundaries in place?

What new boundaries are you willing to set and live by?

Commitment

What are you committed to change to have effective boundaries?

What will have to change to increase your level of commitment to strong boundaries?

Blocks to Success

What is your most ineffective boundary?

Where are you inconsistent regarding your boundaries?

Where are you creating pain in your life by not having solid boundaries?

Where do you benefit by not having effective boundaries?

In what ways do your ineffective boundaries affect other people in your life?

Quantum Thinking

What new boundary do you yearn for in your heart?

What boundaries have you yet to develop that will increase your effectiveness?

What is the boundary that when you set it up and live by it, will take your life to a completely new level?

Actions

What are three actions you will take this week to have effective boundaries in place?

Support

Who do you know who has strong boundaries and would be willing to mentor you?

What support group can you find in your area to help you maintain effective boundaries?

To receive additional information and support, visit Kenneth D. Foster's Living Rich Coaching Community at www.PremierCoaching.com and www.GreatestYearEver.com.

CLEANING THE CLUTTER

*Order doesn't start with an outer action, but with
a vision of symmetry that is set up from within.*

—Kenneth D. Foster

I am amazed by the number of times I meet with clients and we're discussing what they think is holding them back from really creating success in their lives and they tell me it is because they are overwhelmed. But once we dig in, there is so often one common denominator at the root of what is holding them back: Clutter!

Clutter in the workspace, clutter on the kitchen table, in the closets, clutter underneath the bed, in the car, clutter in the basement . . . clutter everywhere! Do you know where clutter starts? In your mind. It is a symptom of an unruly mind. What is showing up in your environment starts first in your mind. And it starts many times with the questions you ask and choices you make.

Many people keep clutter in their lives because they ask poor questions. Questions like "Should I save or keep this magazine, file folder, picture, discount coupon, and so forth, or not?" Remember, the answer is in the question you ask. So, if you ask a poor question like the one just asked, you will get answers like "Maybe, I don't know, or let me think about it," or the most classic answer of all, "You never know, I might need this some day."

These answers lead to confusion and indecision, which is the main reason people can't get rid of their clutter. They don't have a clear understanding of what to do with it. So, to clean up a messy environment, you will have to take back control of your thinking by asking questions that will direct the focus of your mind to come up with an empowering answer.

Try asking questions like "What is the system I can come up with to always have a clutter-free environment?" Or "What has to happen for me to live clutter-free?" Or "What three steps can I take daily to live clutter-free?" By asking these types of questions you will be getting answers that will solve your problem rather than increase the clutter.

Consider this: If you haven't used something in a very long time, if you haven't worn that shirt, opened that book, or spent that coupon, chances are it has outlived its usefulness to you. You no longer need it. It's time to let it go.

The social scientists tell us that the subconscious mind keeps track of every piece of paper and every object in your environment. Have you ever had an uneasy feeling or maybe the feeling of being overwhelmed when you looked at a messy office or house? If so, then you have experienced the results of clutter.

It's so easy to let clutter pile up. In fact, in the short term, it seems easier to just let it build, rather than taking the time and energy to do something about it. Did you know that the number one reason that clutter builds up is from the inability to make a quick decision? That's right. When you are consistently uncertain or doubtful, the result will be clutter. So clutter is actually a mirror of the places in your mind where you are struggling with doubt. Instead of tossing one more magazine onto the pile, start by asking yourself, "Where in my life am I feeling uncertainty, and what has to happen to move past it?"

Think about it. Have you ever sorted through the mail and couldn't make a choice of whether to throw out a piece or save it, so you set it aside for later? Or you come back from a meeting with a folder full of notes but don't have a good place to file it, so it sits? Or you hold on to old items that no longer serve any purpose, but you are afraid to let them go because you think you will need them someday in the future? And then all the stuff seems to somehow multiply, until you've got yourself . . . a pile of clutter!

While just letting things pile up might seem like the easy way in the moment, in the end, you will need a lot of energy to get rid of the junk. It has been said that our environment is more powerful than our own willpower. If you don't believe this, then try to be upbeat and filled with positive energy on a consistent basis in a cluttered room.

Set your intention to create a clutter-free environment and watch your creativity and energy soar. Clutter needs to be dealt with right from the start—before it takes over. It's important to be in charge of clutter, rather than it being in charge of you! Holding on to clutter is like carrying around a 50-pound weight. Is this the way you want to go through life?

Remember that whatever clutter you might have in your life didn't build up overnight, so it will take some time to deal with it all once you decide to roll up your sleeves and dig in. You may want to try using this acronym: F. A.D. When a new piece of mail or information comes in, "File it," "Act on it," or "Discard it."

As you journey through the process of clearing the clutter, create some one-on-one time with yourself and read through the following questions. Choose the ones that resonate with you most and go deep. Ask yourself what's at the root of your clutter . . . and then answer each question in this section until you determine what has to happen for you to leave clutter behind.

Cleaning the Clutter

Evaluation

What do you like about your environment?

What do you want to change in your environment?

What are you tolerating in your environment?

What are the five most distressing areas of clutter you would like to be done with now?

Vision

What does freedom from clutter feel like to you?

What will really make you happy and content with regard to your environment?

What do you want your home and office to look like?

What systems will you put in place to remain clutter free?

Goals

What specific goals will you set to create a beautiful, clutter-free environment?

Purpose

What can you learn from letting go of the clutter?

What is the most important reason for letting go of clutter?

What will you gain by clearing all the rooms in your home of all their clutter?

How will letting go of clutter serve you and your family?

Who will be most proud when you let go of your clutter?

Commitment

What are you committed to doing about your clutter?

Blocks to Success

What has stopped you in the past from letting go of clutter?

What objects from the past no longer define who you are in the present?

What is it costing you to keep clutter in your life?

In what ways do you benefit by keeping clutter in your life?

What are you holding on to inside that is creating clutter on the outside?

Quantum Thinking

What types of thoughts will bring you freedom from clutter forever?

What are you willing to give up to clear all the rooms in your home of all their clutter?

Actions

What action steps can you take to clear all the rooms in your home of all their clutter?

Support

Who is the most organized person you know who would be willing to help you clear your environment of clutter?

What books can you read about cleaning up the clutter?

What coaches or mentors can you contact to help you live a clutter-free existence?

To receive additional information and support, visit Kenneth D. Foster's Living Rich Coaching Community at www.PremierCoaching.com and www.GreatestYearEver.com.

ORGANIZATION

*A calm and organized mind creates a calm
and organized life.*
—Kenneth D. Foster

Ah yes, organization! Maybe you're thinking "How boring. Do I really want to work on organization? Come on, not that!" When you realize, however, that our lives are dictated by the environment we set up for ourselves, and the more organized we are, the happier we can be, this isn't such a bad topic.

Organization is related to efficiency and productivity and also to simplicity and to our ability to live peacefully with ease and grace. When I speak of organization, I won't be talking about setting up complicated systems for running your life. We will be discussing how to organize your life so that you'll have more of what you really want in your life.

Organization is important to me because I am more productive when I'm organized, which results in me creating more wealth, which in turn gives me more time to play. I'm able to be a multitasker without getting stressed out. It bring more beauty in my life because when I am organized, my office *looks* better and it's more pleasing to the senses; it's easier to find things, and it actually creates more joy in my life.

Since organization often relates to getting tasks done and accomplishing goals, one of the biggest obstacles to organization is procrastination. We fall into procrastination for a variety of reasons. Here I'm going to focus on just a few. The first one is the issue of making commitments to yourself. Committing yourself to something and then not following through is the surest way to propagate the procrastination circle. How do you feel when you don't follow through with a commitment? Self-deflated, disappointed, flustered, hopeless, overwhelmed, even angry? Procrastination brings on those feelings, and they're there for a reason.

The negative feelings tell you there is something off-kilter in your life. So, if you are experiencing this, go back and ask yourself, "What am I committed to?" and "What am I willing to do to blast past procrastination forever?" Often, the best way out of the procrastination trap is begin committing to small actions and then resolve to follow through no matter what comes up to block you. We can begin then to feel better about ourselves. Recognizing that your failure to keep a commitment in the past has given you negative feelings is a *good* thing because it guides you to get back on track, one small step at a time.

A second reason many people procrastinate and don't get organized is because they *over*-commit. If you've committed yourself to too many things, resulting in the feeling that you just cannot get everything done even if you worked at it 24/7, then you need to start setting some boundaries. Ask yourself, "What do I get out of being so committed to too many things? Why would I do that?" When you see that you're procrastinating because you have overcommitted, then you'll understand that the pain or frustration you're feeling is the signal to you that it is time to stop this pattern.

At the same time, you may have a value that tells you that you like to give to people. So overcommitting is causing you pain on one hand but appears to be aligned with your value of giving on the other hand—this creates ambivalence. And ambivalence leads to procrastination. Now you can say, "Wait a minute, that's not how I want to live my life," and you start asking yourself some questions such as those in this chapter to help you bring an organizing principle to your commitments (and to letting the over-commitments go so that you can focus on what's most important to *you*.)

Fear is another emotion that keeps us in procrastination and away from organization. We might fear failure, so we cope with that by making ourselves so disorganized that we don't get anything done. Then we can blame time for our failure instead of ourselves "I had so much to do, I just couldn't get to it; I didn't have time, people expect too much of me." In other words, procrastination wreaks havoc with your organizational abilities and seemingly protects you from the failure you fear by making it likely that you *will* fail but you'll have a good excuse—our subconscious mind can get so convoluted sometimes! Or it may be success that you fear. If you're afraid to stand out, afraid of what people might think of you if you let your talents shine in the world, then you may create an aversion to success and use procrastination and lack of organization to sabotage you. Again, another convoluted self-defensive tactic from the subconscious mind.

Procrastination, the bane of organization, is a habit. And any habit takes discipline to break. If you are in the habit of not being organized, here is the process for breaking that habit. Number one, set an intention to break the habit. Number two, ask where you can get pertinent information about breaking the habit—read about it and talk to other people who have broken the habit. Number three, set the date that you are going to start breaking that habit forever. Number four, find somebody—a mentor, coach, or friend—who will hold you accountable for breaking the habit. Five, take daily action toward reversing the habit. You don't have to do it all at once. Just come at it in a consistent and organized way and you'll be amazed at the results.

You create organization with daily action. You make a choice each day with your actions to be either organized or disorganized. For example, in my own life, I don't let mail pile up for two or three days. I deal with it every day. I'll handle mail in the morning, and organize it into bills, accounts receivable, junk mail, and personal mail.

Set up systems that support you staying organized. For example, at the beginning of each year, my wife gets a calendar and first writes out all the spiritual holidays for the entire year. Then she marks off all our family vacations, birthdays, and celebrations. After that, we talk about the workshops we'd like to attend and any other special events. We stay organized and create a balance between our work lives and our personal lives by putting things on a calendar, which shows us where commitments may be getting too piled up. By mapping out our year ahead of time, we protect ourselves from overcommitment and stay on track.

Computers are great organizational tools as well. You can have a calendar reminder function on your e-mail program. You can carry your schedule with you in a smartphone or other handheld computer or cell phone configuration. Or if you like the feel of a book in your hands, you can go with a good, old-fashioned daybook.

Organization has advantages. For example, airline reservations. If you book your flight a month ahead, you're likely going to get the flight time you want, a good seat, and a good price. If you wait until two days before your flight to do the booking, chances are you're going to be flying longer, because you will have stopovers, get a less conveniently located seat, and pay a much higher price.

It's the same with housework or office organization. At home, my wife and I go once a month through all the extraneous stuff that has accumulated and we let it go. We do a major cleaning every spring or early summer and then again in the fall; this is easier to do because we've been doing the monthly organizing. If you allow magazines and newspapers to come into your home or office and you don't have a system for getting rid of them, or all the boxes from suppliers in your business, or all the tin cans that need to be recycled, things are going to pile up.

Organization is not about being rigid. It's about recognizing the ebb and flow of stuff into your life and back out again. It's about you controlling that ebb and flow in a way that makes your life and your work easier.

Organization starts in your mind with the questions you ask yourself about what is most important to you and where you need to draw boundaries. Organization keeps you in the flow. A river flows well because it's contained by riverbanks. If it overflows, what happens? You get a flood. It's the same with your life. By being well organized, you allow the river of your life to flow smoothly and you don't have to worry about being overwhelmed (flooded). Organization is not boring at all. It's a tool that takes you to a more empowered life.

Organization

Evaluation

> What are your greatest strengths around being organized in your life?
> Where has procrastination fit into your life?
> What does being overorganized look like to you?
> What is your organizational philosophy?
> What does being organized mean to you?
> What messages do you send yourself about being organized?

Vision

> What will your home, office, and life look like when you are completely organized?
> What new systems will you incorporate to stay organized?

Goals

> What are your highest goals to get you organized?

Purpose

> How will being entirely organized affect your life?
>
> What about organization is important to you?

Commitment

> What has to happen to make organization your first priority?
>
> What do you need to become organized?

Blocks to Success

> What things are you not going to do with regard to organization?
>
> What excuses are you using to fall short of your organizational goals?
>
> What has stopped you in the past from being organized?

Quantum Thinking

> What thinking can you change inside yourself to become organized in your outer world?
>
> What new beliefs could create a new destiny for you?
>
> In what areas are you not organized now, but when you get organized, will make a profound difference in your life?

Actions

> What measurable results will you achieve when you have become organized?
>
> What three steps can you take this week to become organized?
>
> What are 10 things you can do to become organized?

Support

> Who do you know who can help you get organized?
>
> Where can you find organizational help on the Internet?

To receive additional information and support, visit Kenneth D. Foster's Living Rich Coaching Community at www.PremierCoaching.com and www.GreatestYearEver.com.

SECTION 3

Questions to Bring You What You Want

DREAMS

*To set yourself free, you must give yourself permission
to dream bigger than you have ever dreamed before.*

—Kenneth D. Foster

Dreams—we all have them. They begin in childhood and might come in the form of wanting to be an astronaut, or wanting to build houses, or raise four children, or be a professional baseball player, or star in movies. How wonderful it is to have the mind of a child where *anything* is possible! Of course, you can be an astronaut and travel to the moon. Of course, you will marry well and become wealthy. Of course, you will always be playful and happy. *Why not?!*

And then something happens. We grow older and become influenced by the voices of reason of our parents and teachers. Or other kids tease us and make fun of our dreams, so we gradually just stop talking about them. We begin to develop our own self-imposed limitations and sooner or later many of us are convinced that we're not smart enough, tall enough, strong enough, or cool enough to be that astronaut, become wealthy, and remain playful. And so the dream dies. And a piece of us dies with it, too.

Dreams keep us alive. Dreams give us energy and fuel our passions. Dreams sustain us and give us hope. What most people don't know is that dreams make us uniquely who we are because when we pursue our dreams we become stronger, wiser, and more compassionate as we move past the obstacles to manifesting our dreams.

Whatever your dream is, believe you're entitled to it! It's yours! Believe you deserve it. If for some reason you don't feel entitled to your dream or that you deserve it, then go within and make a list of 25 reasons why you can indeed own that dream! If someone told you that you can't have this or that, stop listening to that voice and instead listen to the voice of what *is* possible.

Everything you see around you was once a dream. When we are children, we think like a child, and have wants or desires of a child. As we grow and understand the power of a dream to shape a life, it is important to understand how dreams work so that we choose our dreams wisely.

My father, Donald J. Foster, recently gave me a very special lesson of how dreams work. He invited me to his home and told me he had a special gift for me. Shortly after I arrived he pulled out the gift and placed it in the palm of my hand. I looked at it, heavy in my palm, weighing close to a quarter pound. It appeared to be an antique, which he later told me was 74 years old. As I looked at this small gift in my hand I wondered how this affected his life, and how would it affect mine?

So I asked, "Dad, what is the story behind this gift?" He said, "When I was about nine years old, I was living in the Chicago area with my family. We didn't have much back in those days. We lived in a one-room apartment above the flower shop where your grandmother was employed. One day, I went to a local store and saw the greatest toy I had ever seen. It moved me and I knew I had to have it. It was a blue motorcycle with a policeman riding it and a side car attached, and on the side of the motorcycle gas tank it had capital letters that read 'COP.' I couldn't believe my eyes. I had to have this toy."

My dad went on to say, "I ran home and asked for the money to buy the toy. Things were tight, but my mom finally gave in and gave me the money to buy it. Little did my parents know at the time, this was going to be my destiny. Every day I could hardly wait to play with this toy, and act out my dream of being a policeman. I played often with this toy for many years. And now I am giving it to you."

I looked at the toy and then I got it! One more time, the lesson of how we manifest in the world was very clear to me.

First, my father was aware of his environment and found the object of his desire, the toy policeman. Next, he envisioned himself being a policeman with all the adventure and excitement it would entail. He did this often and by doing so he planted seeds in his consciousness with the thoughts of being a policeman. Next, he connected to the feeling of what it would be like to be a policeman—happy, excited, joyful, and filled with adventure. Remember, emotion creates *motion*. My dad fully associated himself with the emotions of being a policeman and he took consistent actions when he became of age to make the dream a reality. He used his thoughts, convictions, and emotions to make it happen.

Yes, this is what he wanted to do when he grew up, and he did. His dream came true.

My father served as a Lieutenant Detective for the Los Angeles Police Department for over 48 years. He received many honors during his career, including the Medal of Valor for saving a family from a burning building. He had a passion for being a policeman that most people could never understand. He loved his job. He loved going to work. In fact, he missed fewer than 10 days of work over that 48-year career! His dream kept expanding throughout his career as he worked as a beat cop, then jail duty, then as a detective in the vice, rape, and homicide departments. He learned all aspects of the career, eventually retiring and opening his own detective agency.

So how can *you* make your dreams come true? First, you must get in touch with what you really want. A good way to do this is to ask, "If I could have anything I wanted in the world, what would it be?" or "What would I dare to dream if I knew I could not fail?" Then make a list of those dreams. Just let your creativity flow. Remember, the answers are in the questions you ask, so don't limit yourself in any way, and soon, just like my father did when he first spotted the toy policeman riding the motorcycle, you too will start to see your dreams come true.

Now take some time to answer the questions in this section and make your dreams come alive!

Dreams

Evaluation

What will your legacy be?

What is your greatest advantage in life?

What is perfect about where you are in your life right now?

What is it about you that makes what is showing up in your life inevitable?

What can you accomplish when you dare to dream?

What can you do to expand your dreams?

Vision

What is the most enjoyable dream you have ever had?

Where do your beliefs reflect your dreams?

What do you want to hope for?

What is your dream for the rest of your life?
What does your ideal life look, sound, and feel like?

Goals

How do your dreams relate to your goals?

Purpose

What is the value to you to really create the life of your dreams?
What would you need to really believe in to live the life of your dreams now?

Commitment

What are you willing to give or give up to have the life of your dreams?
What commitment would it take for you to use your mind, imagination, and emotions to create your greatest dreams?

Blocks to Success

What dream or dreams have you given up on?
To what extent do you believe that where you are now in your life is where you are destined to remain?
What has stopped you in the past from living the life of your greatest dreams?
When you believe that you can't have what you want, how do you feel about yourself?

Quantum Thinking

If you could have anything at all, what would it be?
What would you dare to dream if you knew you could not fail?
If the range of possibilities for you is limitless, then what is attainable for you in your lifetime?
What has to happen for you to expand yourself beyond what you think is currently possible?

Actions

What are the five steps you can take this week to move into the life of your dreams?

Support

> Who can you ask today to coach you into living your dreams? Who do you know who can help you put a success team or a mastermind group around you?

To receive additional information and support, visit Kenneth D. Foster's Living Rich Coaching Community at www.PremierCoaching.com and www.GreatestYearEver.com.

GOAL SETTING

No one can predict how great your life will be, not even you, until you choose to be great by setting goals and achieving them.

—Kenneth D. Foster

There's a lot of buzz these days around goal-setting. So, what exactly is a goal? Well, in his best-selling book, *The 7 Habits of Highly Effective People*, Stephen Covey explains that when broken down into its components, a goal turns out simply to be "a dream with a deadline." Once we set a deadline or time frame around a dream, and are fully committed, magical things start to happen.

For example, one of my clients, Shawn (not her real name), had a dream of leaving her long-time corporate job and launching her own coaching business. We used the power of questions to ask her way into her dream. We worked together on a clear vision for that dream: What the business looked like, how it would feel to be self-employed, what the home office setup would be like, how much income the business would generate, how she would market herself—we talked about all the concrete steps. Who did she know who could help her get started, what partnerships were needed to create along the way, and what obstacles might get in the way of her success? This dream soon began to take shape and develop a life of its own!

As most of us know, a dream remains just a dream when we don't act, so Shawn focused her energy and laid out a plan of action. In life, you get what you ask for, right? Well, asking pointed questions about how to create a successful business became all-consuming for her, which really lit a fire under her. The more she asked, the more she visualized the dream in the present tense (feeling as though it had already happened), the more it became a reality and less of being just a dream.

My client is now living her dream and has a very successful coaching business. And that is because she dared to expand the questions she asked. She questioned why this dream was important to her and what she wanted from it. From there, she made it a priority, developed a plan, and made it happen.

It's important to check in with yourself and decide on what's most important in your life. Goals should be chosen on the basis of your unique values. In other words, a good goal is one that is derived from something that is important to you. I recommend you don't do this step lightly. If you are ready to change directions and set new goals, the chances of you succeeding go up dramatically if you are clear with the underlying purpose of attaining your goals. With many of my clients, I will have them write out 25 reasons that they will accomplish their goals.

What I have found over the years is that rarely is it the first or second reason that is important enough to keep the client on track when things get tough. If you are stretching yourself to do things that you haven't done in the past, challenges will surface, so you need to stay very connected to your purpose.

For example, you value having a healthy and fit body, so you set a goal to lose 20 pounds by working out three times a week. You take some time to write out why it is important for you to accomplish this goal. You come up with the facts that you will be able to fit into your clothes, you will feel better about yourself, you will live longer and be there for your children, and you will have fewer doctor bills. Great, you are on the right track! On the contrary, a not-so-good reason for losing 20 pounds would be because your co-worker just lost 20 pounds and you want to keep up with him. Not quite so motivating. In the latter instance, when you are tempted to eat a dessert that has been placed in front of you, you will probably cave in and eat it. Does this make sense to you? I hope so. Why don't you commit right now to never again set goals unless you do the inner work and find out why it is important for you to accomplish them? If you do, you will complete more of your goals and your life will change for the better.

Once you decide which goals you want to set (again, those based on your values), the next important step is to chunk the goal down into manageable, bite-sized bits that feel realistic and doable, and then transfer those steps into your planner or calendar. For example, let's again take the goal of losing 20 pounds to be healthier. Broken down, it might mean that each week you schedule your workouts in your calendar and set aside time for grocery shopping and meal planning so that you are set up for success during the week. Then, ask yourself each day, "What is the one thing I can do today that will help me move toward my goal?"

We start out as children with all kinds of dreams for our big life. But these dreams have been put aside many times for any number of reasons. This doesn't have to be the case for you. Right now you are equipped with the tools necessary to put those past dreams into action! It's exciting what can come true in your life when you simply put your mind to it. So, for a moment, take a ride back to childhood and remember some of those dreams you had. For the ones that no longer fit, leave them behind. But for the ones that are still there and do not seem to go away, it's time to do some checking in with yourself!

We are here on earth to fulfill our destinies and live our dreams by setting goals to reach them. Ponder the questions that follow and get real with your dreams . . . if you dare! Believe it or not, you can accomplish anything—yes, anything—that you put your mind to. Enjoy the ride!

Goal Setting

Evaluation
What has worked for you when setting goals?
What is the most important goal you have set and completed?
Where does goal setting give you an advantage?
What are your beliefs around goal setting?
What do you want to change about the way you set and complete goals?

Vision
What are the top five goals in your life?
By accomplishing your goals, in what areas will your life be different?
What will you realize when you have accomplished your goals?
What could you choose to believe to consistently achieve your goals?
In what ways would your quality of life substantially increase if you completed your goals?

Goals
Which goals will give you the greatest satisfaction when they are accomplished?
What two goals can you set today that will improve your goal-setting performance in the future?

Purpose

> Why is it important for you to set and accomplish your goals?
>
> What about goal setting is important to you?

Commitment

> What is the feeling you are committed to experiencing when you accomplish the goals on your list?
>
> What has to happen for you to be absolutely certain of completing your goals?
>
> What goals have you been putting off that you will to commit to completing?

Blocks to Success

> What has not worked for you when setting goals?
>
> What patterns of action might prevent you from reaching your goals?
>
> In what ways do you benefit by not accomplishing your goals?
>
> What has stopped you from setting and completing goals in the past?

Quantum Thinking

> What do you believe is the secret to setting and accomplishing goals?
>
> What goals are you committed to setting that will completely transform your life for the better?
>
> If you knew for certain that every goal you set would be accomplished, what would your life be like?

Actions

> What new patterns of actions do you need to establish to reach your goals?
>
> What incompletes in your life would a plan of action help you complete?
>
> What are the three actions that you are committed to taking that will help you set and complete your goals from here on out?

Support

> What books can you read that will help you accomplish your goals?

What three friends can you ask to support you in setting and carrying out your goals?

To receive additional information and support, visit Kenneth D. Foster's Living Rich Coaching Community at www.PremierCoaching.com and www.GreatestYearEver.com.

COMMITMENT

If you want to accelerate your rate of achievement, you must ask new questions, explore new commitments, and take daily focused actions until success is achieved.

—Kenneth D. Foster

In this section we look at what you're committed to achieving. If you want to know what you're committed to, take a look at the results that are showing up in your life. If there's anything that you want, any goal you want to reach, you must be fully committed. Think about this. Commitment equals freedom. If you are looking to be free from financial issues, relationship challenges, health problems, worry, stress, poor habits, and so on . . . your commitment will strongly determine what happens.

Before you determine your commitments, you should know what your priorities are, and make sure your commitments match up to those priorities. Let's say you dislike working overtime and value having Fridays off. But you continue to take on tasks and responsibilities that lead you to work longer hours, along with most Fridays. The results you are getting in your life show that you are in fact actually *committed* to working overtime. And in this case, your commitment would not be matching your priorities.

Many of us are never really taught the skills of how to effectively say no. But did you know that every single time you say no . . . you are actually saying "Yes!" to something even bigger and more important? For example, in the scenario just described, saying no to an extra project that would surely lead to overtime is actually saying "Yes!" to quiet time at home, a family outing, getting to bed earlier, time on the lake, or whatever it might be . . . you name it. Look at what you are saying yes to on a daily basis. You are always voting with your power of choice. You are either voting for an outstanding life or a mediocre one.

Of course, we can't make appropriate commitments in our lives if we don't understand our priorities. So, what is most important to you? Once you determine this (Fridays off, losing weight, vacation, family, golf, and so on), then, and only then, can you effectively choose which commitments you would like to make.

As you probably realize, most commitments seem easy to make at the outset (after all, they're simply a verbal or mental acknowledgment of something you say you'll do), but where the work comes in is in the follow-through . . . which is what ultimately produces—or doesn't produce—the results for good in our lives.

There are commitments we make to others, and then there are the commitments we make to ourselves. So many clients I've talked to are stellar at keeping their commitments with others, but fall short when it comes to keeping commitments with themselves. Why is this? It is because of two reasons: They have no accountability to themselves, and they have not determined what it will mean to them in the long run.

When we make a commitment to someone else (such as finishing a project on time), that person will be expecting us to follow through on our word. When we make a commitment to ourselves, though (losing five pounds in 30 days, for example), no one is watching . . . or so we think.

The truth is that we know whether or not we are keeping our commitments. In fact, if we don't lose the five pounds (or say no to it), we have not only violated our commitment to ourselves, but we are in a sense saying yes to something else instead (in this case, saying yes to carrying around extra weight on our bodies) and unconsciously making that a bigger priority.

Remember, you cannot do it all. There is no such thing as a person who can do everything. You have to make choices. You want to make sure that your choices are aligned with your deepest values. If you make a choice and don't do it, you're sabotaging yourself. That's what self-sabotage really is—you think you're saying yes to something but you're really saying no to it. When you find yourself in a situation where part of you says yes and another part of you says no, that's called ambivalence. There's always a lesson in ambivalence. Start asking yourself some key questions to uncover the cause of the ambivalence, because staying in ambivalence keeps you uncommitted.

It is important to note that the psychologists tell us that the primary way to build self-confidence and self-esteem is by making commitments and keeping them. The opposite is also true! If you make commitments and then don't follow through, you will tear down your self-confidence. Do this over and over again, and you will end up with low self-esteem.

So, the commitments we make and keep in our life are directly related to the results we get or don't get. Spend some time asking about what's most important in your life, what commitments you currently have, and what commitments you would like to make. The questions that follow will give you valuable insight on how you are using or not using the power of commitment and help you get in touch with how your commitments are currently working or not. Once you answer the questions in this section, be prepared to tap into the unlimited power that commitments have in store for you!

Commitment

Evaluation

What are you currently committed to in your life?
What are your most significant commitments?
In what areas of your life can you perfect your follow-through?

Vision

What are your highest priorities?
What characteristics will you develop to be able to easily obtain what you desire?
Imagine yourself keeping all your commitments. What will your life look like then?

Goals

What are the goals you have set to obtain or grow your highest priorities?

Purpose

What have you learned about making commitments that will ensure that you will keep your commitments in the future?
Why are you determined to follow through on your commitments?

Commitment

What are your primary commitments for the day, week, month, and year?
What do you need to develop inner certainty that you will fulfill your commitments?

Blocks to Success

What agreements have you made with yourself and broken?
What has stopped you in the past from honoring your commitments?

What does it cost you to not follow through on your commitments?

Quantum Thinking

What would you have to believe about yourself to set commitments and consistently realize them?

What is the highest commitment you could make that would make a difference in the lives of others?

What new commitments will you make that will fast-forward your life to accomplish your dreams?

What thoughts would empower you to always fulfill your commitments?

Actions

What has to happen for you to consistently keep commitments to yourself?

What actions can you take to maintain focus on keeping your commitments?

Support

Who do you know who is respected for keeping their commitments that you can ask to mentor you?

What friends or associates can you ask to give you the names of the best books available about keeping commitments?

To receive additional information and support, visit Kenneth D. Foster's Living Rich Coaching Community at www.PremierCoaching.com and www.GreatestYearEver.com.

SUCCESS

Environment is stronger than most people's will, but faith coupled with resolve will conquer all.

—Kenneth D. Foster

It's easy in this culture of consumerism and quick fixes to measure success by externals—your car, your house, your clothes, your money. But *real* success, like anything else worthwhile in life, begins on the *inside* and is not about appearances.

I define success as freedom—freedom from financial worries, freedom to have positive relationships, freedom to do what you dream about, freedom to live where you want to live, freedom to experience your creator, freedom to create the conditions in your life that have the most meaning for *you* and freedom to realize your full potential. What I encourage you to do is to begin asking yourself some deep questions about what *your* freedom looks like and feels like.

Are you a person who follows your intuition? Intuition is the ability to understand in a very profound way what your heart and spirit is telling you, and it is key to success. Intuition has been overtaken these days by far too much rationality and too much mind analysis, so much so that many people today never take the time to ask themselves, "How do I *feel* about this?," "What is my heart saying?," "What gut level feeling do I have about this particular direction in my life?" The questions in this section are designed to help you do that.

Intuition brings you to self-trust, trusting yourself enough to know that the answers to your success are within you. Self-trust also has a lot to do with the thought habits we form and the willpower we bring to translating our thoughts into action. Nothing undermines self-trust more than making a commitment to oneself and setting goals, and not following through with it. That causes us to start with the negative self-talk—"I guess this isn't possible, after all"—and we find ourselves on a track leading us away from the very success we yearn for.

One way to help you keep your commitments to yourself and your success is to do things in small steps in the beginning. Decide upon an action that you can do *at this very moment*, and do it. No matter how small it seems, the very fact that you completed it increases the voice of intuitive guidance within you. You gain success one step at a time.

If your life right now is not what you want it to be, ask yourself "What would my core beliefs have to be to create the current lifestyle I'm living?"

This question will uncover negative beliefs such as "I'm not worthy," "I can't do that," "I've failed before," "I tried but I ended up losing my shirt," "I'll never succeed." All these messages from the past that keep playing out in the present just below the surface of your mind are like a radio station you've turned down really low but its murmurs still persist in getting through to your psyche.

Funny thing about failure. There are some wise mentors out there who say, "Increase your failure to increase your success." That's just a way of saying that if you're not willing to risk failure, you're not going to achieve success. Success means taking a chance on something, going for it, even if you're not sure how it's going to come out. Failure is not a negative. It's merely a signpost to take a different direction.

There have been many times in my own business when we decided to try something new that nobody had done before, and we failed. When we first started doing teleclasses back in 2000 at a time when very few companies were offering conference call services, we didn't have much experience. The first teleconference had only 10 people. We were anticipating over 100. It would have been easy to give up at that point and say, "So much for that!" But we chose instead to persist, and this involved many failures. We went through several assistants, had to try out different conferencing services, figure out the right match for the company, and went down many wrong paths. But we kept on, and last year we did a teleconference with over 7,000 participants on the line. Today, we have become one of the largest teleconferencing companies in the personal and professional development business.

I learned another key lesson about success when I was involved with a 100-mile bike race some years ago. I had searched out an organization called Team In Training. They told me that if I raised $2,500 for them, they would teach me how to ride a 100-mile race. At the time, I had never raised that amount of money for a charity. I didn't have a bike and I didn't know much about racing. I found a bike on the Internet, a Trek bike, and paid $400 for it. On the first day I got together with the team, they decided to take us 25 miles. I knew this would be a large stretch for me because I hadn't ridden 25 miles on a bike before without stopping! They taught us all the hand signals, showed us how to avoid obstacles in the road, where to stop, when to move up behind someone. I was really enthusiastic as we started. Within a half hour or so, I succeeded in moving myself up to the front of the pack. I really liked having the lead and was pedaling pretty hard. Pretty soon I was getting tired. I had to contend with the wind rushing at me from the front, and so I figured I should drop back behind the others for a while. So I gave the hand signal to drop back in the pack, and as soon as I was at the back of the pack, I had a realization that what I had been doing in my life up until that point was the wrong way to do life!

The enlightened moment was *this*—when I got to the back of the pack of 16 riders, there was no wind. I was actually being pulled along by the team. It dawned on me that in my life I had been letting my ego get too big and I had never really allowed a team to help me. I'd always been the one pulling other people behind me. At that moment, I made the decision to create a good team around me, no matter what I'm doing. I also decided to ask a new question when challenges came up. The question I asked and continue to ask today is, "How is this (circumstance) a lot like my life"? This one question has me looking at outer circumstances that show up daily and helps me become introspective and learn at an incredible pace.

You never succeed alone. It takes other people, combined with your own inner determination and your understanding of your own truest desires, to help you succeed. Know that whatever has knocked you down in the past doesn't mean that you can't get up in the future. There are more roads to your success than you ever dreamed possible. Use the questions in this book to get you there. Team up with your inner self so that you're not always riding into the wind. Let your intuition, your self-trust, and your commitment to your own inner freedom carry you to success.

Success

Evaluation
What is your track record for getting what you want in life?

What is the greatest lesson you have learned about success?

What messages have you been sending yourself regarding your success?

What qualities do you display to the world when you are successful?

Where have you been invincible and victorious in your life?

Vision

    What is your vision for having a super successful life?

    What do you already know that assures you will be successful?

    What would someone who really expects to succeed be doing without a doubt?

    What do you need to really trust yourself to succeed?

Goals

    What will happen when you become determined to achieve your goals?

    What are your top five goals to creating success in your life?

Purpose

    When do you feel most successful and why?

    What about success is important to you?

    What would you need to believe to be successful?

    What really defines success for you?

Commitment

    What do you need to accomplish whatever you desire?

    If you are not happy with the results you're getting, what are you willing to change?

    What do you need to increase your desire for success?

Blocks to Success

    What are the personal issues or challenges that are repeatedly blocking your successes?

    What is the payoff for not being successful?

    What fears have stopped you from succeeding in the past?

    If you fail to improve or change, what will that ultimately cost you?

    What questions do you ask yourself that disempower you?

    What beliefs have been holding you back from all the success you deserve?

    What are the signs that you are heading down the path of failure?

Quantum Thinking

    If there were something new that you needed to know to be successful, what would it be?

    What magnificent successes will you create this year?

If you chose to think successful thoughts every moment, how would your life be different?

What would you do with your life if you were brave?

If you believed that you are perfect just the way you are, how would you live your life?

Actions

What must happen for you to incorporate successful traits in your life?

What is your strategic plan to get started on a successful path in your life?

What can you do to transform your problems into solutions?

What will you do today to prepare for success tomorrow?

Support

Who can you meet today who will make a massive change in your success?

Who are three mentors in three different areas of life who you could ask to help you increase your success?

To receive additional information and support, visit Kenneth D. Foster's Living Rich Coaching Community at www.PremierCoaching.com and www.GreatestYearEver.com.

QUANTUM BREAKTHROUGH

To know the thoughts of God is to know how

to succeed in life.

—Kenneth D. Foster

Have you ever been at a place in life where you're feeling completely stuck and then something miraculous happens and you are able to break through all limitations and move to a new level of understanding instantly? This process is called a *quantum breakthrough*.

It's easy to get stuck among those old beliefs that no longer serve you. An example might be that you are in a relationship that feels unsuccessful. The doubt creeps in and you tell yourself, "I don't know enough to be in a great relationship." So what has to happen then? You must actually start asking yourself the right questions to begin to *create* a great relationship. The question becomes, "What would it be like to be in an outstanding relationship?" Stay in that question and be with it. Because you will begin to come up with your own answer that actually *shifts* your perception from what you thought you didn't have to a whole new way of looking at a relationship. You begin to see unconditional love, great communication, someone to nurture and honor. You break through the old and leap into the new!

Another example might be that you are at a point in your life where you are so fed up with your habits and ways of living that you resolve to "never live like this again." Once again, you ask yourself the important question to get you moving: "So what are the values or commitments I will live?" When you make a firm commitment to live in the new way and enlist the actions that will support you, you have had a quantum breakthrough. As soon as we understand that there is a solution for every single problem if we ask the right questions, the quantum breakthroughs begin to unfold. We begin to access thought patterns that are higher than the thoughts we previously had.

While asking the right questions instantly multiplies our personal effectiveness, we can't stop there. We absolutely must follow through with action to seal the deal. So, when we refocus our minds on the questions that help us feel successful and ask ourselves every single day: "What has to happen today for me to feel successful?," at the end of the year you will have asked yourself 365 times. And so each day you'll be following through with doing the things that make you feel successful. As you follow through, you *become* successful. This takes focus and action. Using your mind to ask yourself questions and get the answers, combined with following through in daily action, will get you the right results.

Ultimately, you'll be creating your destiny.

If you're wondering how you begin to create these quantum break-throughs, here's what you need to know. Opening up your mind is a learned skill set. It takes discipline, commitment, and focused action. Find a quiet spot every day (in the morning or evening) and become the observer of your thoughts as you quiet your mind. Once you're there, ask yourself the questions listed on the following pages until you get the answers you *know* are true for *you*. Your subconscious mind cannot answer these questions. You need to access the superconscious mind, where the unlimited source of all answers resides. This is your connection to spirit and wholeness. This is where the world of quantum resides.

Keep asking until you get the answer. Feel it in your heart and in your gut as you look for the truth to help set yourself free from whatever it is you're struggling with. Once you know your truth, the details will follow naturally. You'll have broken through to a whole new reality.

Quantum Breakthroughs

Evaluation

> Where in your life do you need a big breakthrough?
> In what areas of your life are you feeling stuck?
> What is it that you want to achieve, but it isn't happening for you?
> What has kept you believing that you can get what you want?

Vision

> What will bring you permanent victory in whatever area you choose?
> What is life asking you to do differently at this point in your life?
> What does the wisest part of you say will create unlimited success?
> What would your life look like if you released all your self-doubt?
> Where can you find the answers you need to get what you want in life?

Goals

> What goals will you set to establish quantum breakthroughs in your life?
> What are the most important goals you can set this year?

Purpose

What is the key to unleashing your greatness?

Why will you break through any obstacles that are standing in the way of succeeding in all areas of your life?

Commitment

What is the most important commitment you can make to yourself?

What do you need to become committed to succeeding so deeply that nothing can stand in your way?

Blocks to Success

What do you believe is impossible for you to accomplish right now, which, if it were possible, would change your life forever?

What habits are blocking you from having what you want in life?

What are you pretending not to see about your personality that is stopping your success?

Quantum Thinking

What limitations do you believe about yourself that you are willing to doubt?

What do you need to know to enjoy increased power, joy, and financial freedom?

What will bring you freedom from every limitation you have created for yourself?

When you truly know that nothing can prevent you from being free, how will you act?

What one belief could you change right now that will create unending wealth?

What is the next step in your evolution?

What has to happen to celebrate your accomplishments so completely that you disconnect from who you've known yourself to be?

Actions

What resources can you mobilize right now to create massive abundance in your life?

What areas of your life do you intend to change forever in the next two weeks?

What is one thing you can do to make a small change immediately that will create profound long-term results?

Support

Who are your role models who appear to have accomplished the impossible?

Who can support you in setting quantum goals and accomplishing them?

Who is the biggest thinker you know who can help you?

To receive additional information and support, visit Kenneth D. Foster's Living Rich Coaching Community at www.PremierCoaching.com and www.GreatestYearEver.com.

SECTION 4

Questions to Create Financial Freedom

CAREER

To be on fire with the passion of purpose puts joy

in one's work.

—Kenneth D. Foster

One day a few years back, I was roller skating with a group of friends around Mission Bay in San Diego, California. It was a beautiful day; the temperature was around 75 degrees with a light wind blowing across the bay. As we were waiting for a few friends to join our group, we happened upon a young boy with dark brown hair and stellar blue eyes. The first question I asked him was his name and he said, "My name is Alex and I am five years old."

I then asked Alex the standard question that many of us were routinely asked during our childhood, "What do you want to be when you grow up?" When asked this question, Alex paused for several seconds and contemplated his answer. As he pondered, I noticed he had compelled rapt attention from our group and all eyes were on Alex. Then he looked up to the sky and back down, peering deeply into my brown eyes and said, "When I grow up, I just want to be me." Everyone in the group was silent. With those simple words "I just want to be me," he had touched our dreams, ambitions, and our souls.

Some of us had big dreams of owning our own business or being an astronaut, a president, or a millionaire; others simply dreamed about being in service as a teacher, fireman, policeman, missionary, or a parent raising a family. Regardless of the dreams, we have all pondered the question of who we wanted to be when we grew up at some time in our lives. But here in our presence was a five-year-old sage, reminding us to stop and reflect on our life.

What stopped us from pursuing our greatest dreams? Well, many of us had loving, well-intentioned parents, teachers, friends, grandparents, or preachers who influenced us to take a path. But maybe that path didn't match our dreams. They may have said things like, "You need to get a job and make money," or "You should continue to run the family business just as your parents and their parents did," or "You're not smart enough to own a business because you've got only a high school education." Or how about: "You're so good at math! You should really be an accountant."

So often in my coaching practice, I have worked with clients who are doing extremely well in their jobs, getting all sorts of kudos and recognition from their peers . . . only for me to find out that just because they're good at what they do, it doesn't come remotely close to meaning that they like it or enjoy it. It is simple to teach a dog to do tricks and perform for the master, but it doesn't mean that it is in the dog's nature to perform the trick, nor do they enjoy doing them. Does this make sense?

Many times people tend to feel trapped and locked into a specific career. When asked, "What do you love to do?" they will open up and talk about their dreams, which almost never includes what they are doing in the moment. Indeed there have been studies that show that up to 75 percent of people, and possibly more, do not enjoy what they do for a living. What? Only one in four find joy and meaning in their work? What about the other three? I have found that when people disconnect from their dreams and goals, a downward spiral begins, negatively affecting not only them, but their families, peers, and many other areas of their lives. And, it seems, we're increasingly accepting this as the norm. But do we have to?

Our greatest potential for happiness and growth is when we capitalize on our *strengths, abilities, and skills that we are good at.* When we're feeling stuck in a career, it is a sign that it's time to change, and if you don't listen to your heart's calling, then the pain of dissatisfaction will become greater as you wither in your career.

Think about the ways that you are hard-wired. You know, those gifts and talents that innately make up what you are. For example, I have a colleague who literally comes alive when she is in teacher mode; she loves to teach people and help them grow, develop, and learn. I've seen her standing over the shoulder of her colleagues explaining office concepts to them and helping them better understand the way their mailing business runs. Her current career, however, has her placed in a small cubicle in the basement of an office building. When I asked her, "Why are you doing this job?" her reply was that she needs the money. Well, she may need the money, but her passion and skill sets couldn't be further away from what gives her the most energy: teaching people!

What I'm getting at here is that knowing what your greatest talents and abilities are is a great starting point for creating a life filled with passion and joy. After you identify what you're good at and what you *enjoy* doing, then ask, "What has to happen for me to fulfill my greatest dreams?" See how you can either tweak your current career to allow you to do more of what you love doing, or maybe it's time to search out other careers that are more of a match with who you are.

Sadly, many people leave their soul and dreams in the car as they're running into their workplace. They have lost their courage and faith to bring forth their God-given talents. If this has been you in the past, then stop right here and now and commit to reconnecting with your dreams. It can be very simple: just carve out a half hour each day to honestly answer the following questions. There is the right career out there for everyone; you just have to do some digging to understand what is right for you, and then take courageous actions to manifest your dreams.

Career

Evaluation

Is your current career the one you envisioned for your life?
What makes you believe your current career is the one for you?
What is your payoff for staying in your career?
Why did your current and past employers pick you?
What do you love the most about your career?

Vision

What is your ideal career that will bring out the best in you?
What do you love to do?
What are your greatest strengths?
What would you be doing if you knew you could pay the bills and succeed?
If you could change one thing about your career path, what would it be?
What do you believe to be the greatest use of your talents and skills?

Goals

Where can you become more influential in your career?
What skills do you want to learn to enhance your career?
What skill could you develop that would have the most impact on your career?
What are the four goals you will set that will propel your career to new heights?

Purpose

What work do you feel passionate about doing?
What does your career mean to you? What more could it mean?
Why is being in the right career important to you?

What is currently motivating you to excel beyond belief in your career?

Commitment

What do you need to be fully committed to having the career of your dreams?

What are you absolutely committed to having in your career?

What opportunities are you committed to manifesting in your career?

What benefits will you receive committing fully to a single career path?

Blocks to Success

Where are you disillusioned in your career?

What is stopping you from having the career of your dreams?

What holds you back the most in your career?

What is not true about you that prevents you from taking your career to the next level?

What keeps tripping you up in your professional life?

What are you waiting for in your career?

Quantum Thinking

If you could do anything you desired, what career would you choose for yourself?

What kind of performance from you would attract the position of your dreams?

Actions

What three actions could you take this week to advance your career?

What action steps do you need to take this week to surpass all your expectations about your career path?

Support

Who would be an ideal mentor to support you in obtaining the fulfillment you want in your career?

What career counselors or human resource experts can you ask to help you manifest your career goals?

To receive additional information and support, visit Kenneth D. Foster's Living Rich Coaching Community at www.PremierCoaching.com and www.GreatestYearEver.com.

BUSINESS

When your energy, creativity, and enthusiasm become unending, you have found the secret to business success.

—Kenneth D. Foster

If you're a business owner, you probably realize the importance of having your business stand apart from your competition. The odds are, like most business owners, you may not have done the foundational work when you initially set up your business . . . you just kind of dove in. And that's great! But it's imperative that you stand back from your business to gain clarity on several key points so that you can maximize your business success.

Think back to when you first started your business. What were the main reasons you wanted this business? Maybe it was because you had a product or service that the world just had to have. Or maybe you decided you weren't cut out for an office job and you simply had to get out. Maybe you saw unlimited possibilities by being your own boss and you were excited to take the challenge. Whatever the reason, take some time to go back to the beginning and tap into that initial passion or seed thought that fueled you to strive for success. Beware of being one of those business owners who "forgets where he came from and why he's in business." Keep the passion alive!

In addition to remembering the reason you started your business, it's just as important to understand the purpose, or mission, of your business. Big companies spend time on meticulously crafting a mission statement that serves as their true north. When dealing with customers, it's a way of saying, "Here's what we stand for." A mission statement serves as an umbrella for big decisions, too; in other words, everything that a business does is because it somehow falls underneath a greater mission statement. Identify your business's purpose. Your customers need to know who you are and what you stand for.

A mission statement is about values and integrity. It lets your customers know that you are there to give service to them. It's also a constant reminder to you of why you created this business—and we all need these reminders for the times when things get tough. Any successful entrepreneur will tell you that a business has its ups and downs. If you don't have a solid mission statement, you can easily run aground on the shoals of difficulties rather than steering around them.

Once you're clear on the underlying mission or purpose of your company, your ideal clients will want to know how to find you. But, you've got to know who your ideal client is! Think about the type of customer who is absolutely *perfect* for your business. Don't hold back! Lock in to this perfect client. Get a good vision of this person—the problems in her life that she needs solved, the way you can help her, and how you can reach her. The Law of Attraction states that the more you focus on what you want in life, the more you will attract just that. Keep that image of your ideal client at the forefront, don't lose sight of her, and then watch the right business relationships begin to develop.

Environment is often stronger than most peoples' willpower, so look around at your surroundings: Your office space, your colleagues, the employees you hire, the motivational prints on the wall, the successful colleagues who just doubled their income, the reliable and friendly employees who are eagerly ready to go every morning. It's important that everything around you supports your values, mission, and who you are today. Set yourself up for success!

As you take inventory on the foundation of your business, watch for what's working and what's not. It can be so easy to operate on autopilot, not really paying attention to the things that need attention. When you become an expert on taking care of the things that aren't working and focusing your time and energy on the things that *are* working, everyone around you will notice and your business will run much more smoothly.

Clarity is the key, and asking the right questions will help you get clear. Make sure you have clear expectations, clearly outlined job descriptions, and clearly defined goals. Dare to stretch yourself by raising the bar for you and your business! Expect nothing but the best and set goals that will make you ecstatic when you reach them. Remember, this is *your* business and *you* get to call the shots.

Lastly, follow your energy. As the boss, you know best. When a project drains you and gives you no energy, there's a message there for you—usually you are doing something you don't want to be doing. When you feel simply jazzed about a particular business relationship and see the synergy created, there's another message for you. Trust your instincts about your business. Do what you do best and hire the rest!

Now is the time to reflect on the great business you have created. Allow yourself to ponder the following questions to assist you on your path toward greatness.

Business

Evaluation

What are your reasons for being in business?

What is your job description—specifically, what do you get paid to do?

What is the biggest challenge you are facing in your business?

What is exciting about your business?

What is the potential for your business?

Vision

What is the most compelling vision you can create for your business?

What will you accomplish that is way beyond where you are today?

What would your business and personal revenues be in an ideal month?

What amount of time do you want away from your business and when will you take it?

Goals

What are the five most important goals to accomplish this year in business?

What might stop you from achieving those goals?

Purpose

Why is it important that your business succeeds?

What is the purpose of your business?

What principles and values would you like to incorporate into your business?

Commitment

What are you committed to doing, that when you do, will enroll key players in your vision?

What has to happen this week for you to double your commitment to succeed?

Blocks to Success

What are you tolerating in your business?

When does your attitude affect your business in a negative way?

What is taking you off track from having the business of your dreams?

What may stop you from succeeding in your business?

What are the signs that you are heading toward failure in your business?

Under what conditions are you most likely to lose your business edge?

Quantum Thinking

If your business were to be totally aligned with your purpose and your passions, what would your business be like?

What new beliefs will you have to embrace to dramatically build your organization?

What specifically can you do to increase the success of your key leaders?

What can you give your customer that they will value so highly that no competitors could ever keep up?

If you were to take off the limits of your mind, what would be possible for your business?

Actions

What could you delegate to others that would free up your time?

What can you do to create a powerful business team where everyone feels he belongs?

What can you do to double your business prospects within a short time?

Support

What can you do to find key leaders?

Who do you appreciate in your business?

To receive additional information and support, visit Kenneth D. Foster's Living Rich Coaching Community at www.PremierCoaching.com and www.GreatestYearEver.com.

LEADERSHIP

There is no shortage of leaders today—they are everywhere.
But there is a shortage of great men and women who
empower others, are compassionate, and serve the
greater good.

—Kenneth D. Foster

I've studied leadership for many years, as a way of clarifying my own ideas about this very important aspect of human behavior. I've read biographies of many individuals—from the Dalai Lama to Yogananda to Jesus to Caesar to Napoleon to Donald Trump to Tony Robbins—almost every possible leadership style you could imagine.

People have different ways of defining leadership. Some define leadership as a form of charisma, a certain magnetic quality that seems to draw people. Some people see leadership as performing heroic feats. Others see leadership as getting a job done effectively. Some see leaders as being visionaries. Some see leadership as being in charge. Others see leadership as empowering others to make their own individual choices. Some see leadership as a team effort. Others see it as independent action. Some see leadership as being a great orator using words brilliantly. Others see leadership as the ability to sit quietly, saying very little, yet changing the atmosphere in a room with the power of peaceful presence. Leadership can encompass all of these styles and many more.

To me, real leaders understand the dynamics of individuals and groups. And what better way to understand this than by asking questions? This section's questions guide you to explore the leader in you. There is an old saying that leaders are born, not made. I disagree with that idea. All of us have some capacity of leadership within us, and much of leadership is a *learned* skill.

I believe that today's true leaders have at heart the best interests of the communities they serve. They look for the win/win/win in each situation. In a business setting, the company wins, the employee wins, and they win. In a home setting, the family member wins, they win, and the community wins. A true leader doesn't operate on just reason and logic, but also knows how to call upon intuition and to care about more than just the bottom line.

A real leader is a person who can hold a space for others to feel safe to express their thoughts and talents. Far too often, leadership gets unconsciously contaminated with bullying, the my-way-or-the-highway approach. Yet research shows that those kinds of leaders in fact have a detrimental effect on the organizations they lead. Just read any current newspaper today to find multiple examples of how the me-first leadership style destroys the fabric of communities and the sacred trust within society.

A true leader is not "me first." A true leader does take his own needs into account but also strives for balance and commits to holding a standard a group can move toward. Leadership is based on respect, empowerment, clear-sightedness, and compassion.

Unfortunately, being in a leadership position doesn't necessarily mean that a person is a great leader. Current economic and political situations today provide ample examples of blind or misguided leadership. If a leader is not constantly taking steps to improve her own level of awareness, if the leader is not continually asking questions about how to change, develop, and grow, leadership then becomes blind. In my view, a true leader knows how to be introspective—understanding that leadership, like any other worthwhile human quality, begins within.

The more a leader can see his own strengths and shortcomings in a clear light through the process of self-examination, the more the leadership qualities will grow and flourish. These are the leaders the world is calling for. We have settled too often for mediocrity in place of excellence, and as a result of that, we have created a lot of pain and suffering in the world.

It's time to wake up. It's time to bring back the values this nation and most of the free world were founded on. We were founded on spiritual values, on values of freedom, on values of respect, on values of justice. It's all there in the U.S. Constitution (and in the Charters of Rights of many other nations) and we need to get back to those values, start living them, and not accepting anything less from our leaders than that.

Having said that, though, don't just think of leadership as something that only a few elected people do in upholding the values of a nation. The reality is that in some areas of each of our lives, we are *each* a leader. If you're a parent, you're a leader to your children. If you're a doctor, you're a leader to your patients. If you're a manager or business owner, you're a leader to your employees. If you're a Little League coach, you're a leader to your players. If you're the chairperson of a community committee, you're a leader on that project. If you write a letter to the editor of your community's newspaper, you're exercising leadership in expressing your opinions on issues of importance. If you incorporate physical exercise and good nutrition into your life, you're a role model for your family and colleagues in doing the same.

It's true that some people may seem to have more innate talents for leadership, but in reality, whether we have those innate qualities or not, there are times in life when we will *all* be called to leadership of one sort or another. To believe that leadership is only the purview of your boss, or politicians and government, or spiritual leaders like the Dalai Lama or Martin Luther King, is to abdicate the leader within *you*. There are times in your life when you must empower the leader within you to step forward, even in a small way. And a thousand small ways can add up to making a very *big* difference. Lead yourself on—to the questions in this section!

Leadership

Evaluation

> In what ways are you an ideal leader?
> What are your greatest leadership strengths?
> What is the biggest challenge you face as a leader?
> What are the supreme lessons that you have learned as a leader?
> What is your ultimate potential as a leader?

Vision

> What is your ideal leadership role?
> Who are five leaders you admire and what are the values that you will emulate?
> In your view, what are the five greatest attributes of strong leaders?
> What will you strive to achieve as a leader?
> What are the three highest leadership qualities you will consistently exhibit this year?

Goals

> What are three goals that you can set to increase your leadership abilities?

What level of leadership are you ready to step up to and when will it happen?

Purpose

Why is it important for you to be an outstanding leader?

What leadership qualities have you yet to develop that you could use to both help others and better your life?

Commitment

What has to happen to awaken your passion and make leadership a reality for you?

What leadership skills are you committed to developing?

What leadership characteristics are you committed to developing in your personality?

Blocks to Success

What has it cost you to not trust your leadership abilities?

What is your payoff for not moving into a more powerful leadership position?

What must you realize to increase your leadership abilities 10-fold?

What leadership position will you be prevented from achieving if you hold on to your current beliefs?

What factors are preventing you from taking on a more positive leadership role?

Quantum Thinking

What has to happen for you to reawaken your desire to be all you can be?

What can you do to create massive success in all areas of your life?

As a leader, what do you need to consistently align your beliefs and actions?

Actions

What actions will you take in the coming weeks to propel you into the leadership position of your dreams?

Support

What kinds of leadership programs could help you develop yourself as a leader?

Who do you know who could mentor you in becoming a powerful leader?

Who could you invite to be on your dream team of leaders to mentor you on a weekly basis?

To receive additional information and support, visit Kenneth D. Foster's Living Rich Coaching Community at www.PremierCoaching.com and www.GreatestYearEver.com.

MONEY

The answer is in the questions you ask, and the magnitude of your questions will establish the size of your answers. So ask multimillion-dollar questions if you want to get multimillion-dollar answers.

—Kenneth D. Foster

From the time we were young, we learned about money. We might have had an allowance with a specific amount of money we received every week, or set up a lemonade stand with a neighborhood friend to earn some extra change. We watched adults in our world exchanging money for goods, paying bills, earning a living, and sometimes we even saw them fighting over money. Our beliefs and ideas about money started from the very beginning and have shaped our views about money today.

The problem is that for many of us, our money education was not consistent. Our childhood efforts of selling lemonade or spending our allowances were never taken to an adult state. Chances are no one really sat down with us and explained how making a sale on a lemonade stand might relate to the commerce you would perform as an adult. Your parents might have told you that saving your allowance is a good thing, but did anyone take it further and explain, as you grew up, what the principles of sound investment are? And, in particular, if we were given negative beliefs about money—for example, that it's the root of all evil, or people with money are selfish—chances are that you've carried these assumptions around, un-challenged, in your psyche. But these financial attitudes influence you today, and in large part predict how you're doing financially.

Our culture has given rise to many myths about money. One of the most prevalent money misconceptions among some of the people I coach is that there is a lack of money or that money is hard to get. Our society has lots of axioms, like "Money doesn't grow on trees," "You're not made of money," and so on. In other words, many of us have a mindset of scarcity rather than abundance. The truth of the matter is that there is no lack of money in the world. Money is everywhere—trillions of dollars are in circulation all the time. There is no shortage of money, but thinking there is makes it so.

"Yes," you might say, "but that doesn't mean I have enough of it. I just can't seem to get ahead." It's true that many people are struggling financially; it's true that many people have an uncomfortable debt load. But it's important to remember that the way to deal with the issue of money in your life is to approach it from the *inside*, not the outside. If you just focus on external circumstances—the world economy, your own debt load, and so forth, you won't be able to transform your own money consciousness. And it does all begin with consciousness.

The path to financial abundance lies within you. Most important, to find this path to wealth, you have to ask yourself the right questions and tap into your inner truth. By the way, you will know when you have tapped into the truth, because you will most likely have an *aha* moment or feel a shiver run through your body or experience a feeling of certainty.

Ask questions like: What are my greatest natural talents? What are my greatest skills? What are five ways I could begin to create more wealth in my life right now? These questions can seem like surface questions, but they're actually very deep and require a lot of self-reflection.

How do you put a dollar value on your dreams? The answer is you don't. It's great to make a lot of money, but if your focus of life is mainly on dollar figures, you're missing something very crucial. The most abundant life is focused on purpose, not money. If you're in alignment with your truest dreams, and take daily focused actions, the financial resources will follow.

Ask yourself: Why is it important for me to manifest my dreams? Write out 25 reasons why it's important for you to achieve a dream, and don't make any of those answers be about money. You'll uncover the passion inside of you that can then turn those dreams into gold. After you ground yourself in the passion of your dream, at that point you can turn your attention toward the financial goals involved in your dream.

Remember, I'm not telling you to stop having a monetary goal. What I am saying is that to win the game of life and to create the wealth that you are choosing to create, focus first on the reasons for doing it and your passion, then set up your dollar goals, plans, and actions.

The next step is to begin taking action—*daily* action. Ask yourself: What are three actions I can take today that will contribute to creating the amount of money I want? Who are the people I should talk to today? What are 10 different industries that could use my skills? What are 15 ways I could market my talents? What do I need to know to write a good business plan? What do I need to know about investments? How do I develop a wealth consciousness as I pursue my goals?

How *do* we bring in wealth consciousness? By using our thoughts to focus our mind in the direction of our dreams. Are your thoughts about creating wealth or are they thoughts of lack and shortages? As you read these words, you might now be thinking, "Oh, it's fine for Ken Foster to be saying this. After all, he's a successful author with a great business. He doesn't have to worry about putting food on the table."

When it comes to scarcity, I've been there—more than once. I've known what it's like to be down to my last dollar. When you're financially strapped and in danger of losing your home or you can't buy food or clothes, or you've lost your job, or your business has had a setback, the human tendency is to become paralyzed by fear. The fear tells you, "You won't get this," "You can't do that," "You're going to lose everything." I know these thoughts. I've had more than my share of fear-based thoughts in my life.

But what I learned is that fear will never solve a money problem. And so I made the decision in my own life to move from fear to faith—faith in myself, faith that there is an answer to any problem, faith in a higher power that can guide me, faith in my own talents, skills, and gifts. Though there are many challenges that come our way in life, we each have enough hidden strengths within us to overcome all obstacles. If you're in financial trouble right now, ask yourself, "What are some ways I could begin to solve my money issues?" Are there friends or family members you could ask to mentor you? Can you access debt counseling? Can you qualify for a job retraining program? Is there a way you could make your investments more stable? Can you do a comparison between how you're spending the money you do have and what you're earning? Can you make some decisions on how you spend money? On how to save money? Are there expenditures you could eliminate that are not serving you?

Instead of focusing on what's not working in your life, ask yourself, "What is working in my life? What are my strengths? What am I grateful for? What do I need to do to grow in the direction of my dreams?" When you continually ask yourself questions like this, you are leading yourself to success. Ask and you will succeed. It may not be overnight, but you'll be on the right path. There is a Buddhist saying that goes something like this, "If you are heading in the right direction, just keep walking." I would also add to this, "If you are walking in the wrong direction, stop, ask some new questions and find a new direction."

The caveat to all this is that it's not just questions alone. You need to align your questions with *actions* that you'll consistently take on a daily basis to manifest wealth in your life.

Once you begin manifesting wealth in your life, you need to take personal responsibility for managing it. Do you just turn everything over to a financial adviser or stockbroker and forget about it? That would be abdicating your own responsibility. Good financial advisers are useful, but it's up to you to learn about your own investments, about how they work, about the goals you have set, about making wise financial decisions, about assessing the level of financial risk that you can tolerate in your life.

If you're near retirement, it's probably not a good idea to bet the farm on doing a lot of financial speculation (unless you have extra money to play with). Or if you're in debt or raising children, again you might not want to be highly speculative in your investments but adopt a middle road instead. Create some strategies around what you'll accept as your own risk-and-reward ratio. Find a reliable and trustworthy financial adviser to help you do this. Don't be afraid to shop around among the profession of financial advisers, to ask them questions, and check out their qualifications and reputation.

Money strategies can ultimately be very simple—such as putting aside some money every week for savings, even if it's just five dollars to begin with. Taking responsibility for your money actions builds your self-esteem and self-respect and helps you create a place in your heart for success on your own terms. If you really understand who you are, what you're all about, what your values are, what gives you the most meaning in your life (the love, joy, gratitude, and blessings already in your life), the money you make will help more of that come forth. There will be enough. Just tap in to your inner wealth and bring it forth through the questions you ask in this section.

Money

Evaluation

How would you rate your current financial condition?

What have you learned about managing money over the last few years?

What is possible for you financially?

What kind of emergency fund have you established and why?

If your income stopped today, how long could you maintain your lifestyle?

Vision
>
> What is your financial vision for the next five years? (Be specific.)
> How much money do you choose to save each month?
> What will make financial freedom a reality in your life?
> If you suddenly had 50 million dollars right now, what would you be doing differently?

Goals
>
> What are your specific financial goals for the next year? For the next two years? For the next five years?
> How will achieving your financial goals help you live your purpose and your dreams?

Purpose
>
> Why is it important for you to achieve financial freedom?
> What will your life look like at age 75 if you continue on the financial road that you are on today?
> What turns you on about making money?
> Why is it important for you to increase your cash flow?

Commitment
>
> What three commitments are you willing to make to have the money you desire?
> What are you willing to give up to create unending wealth?
> What new financial habits are you willing to put in place?
> What will it take for you to focus on your monetary goals and actually accomplish them?

Blocks to Success
>
> Where will you be financially in one, three, or five years, if you continue doing what you are doing?
> What would a person have to believe to be in your financial situation?
> What has been stopping you from meeting your monetary goals?
> If you could change any habit you have around money, what would it be?
> What is your payoff for falling short of your monetary outcomes?
> What would have to happen for you to make better financial decisions?
> What could possibly block your financial success in the future?
> What have you been putting off doing in regard to your finances?

Quantum Thinking

> What beliefs will you need to change toward yourself and money to free yourself from debt and encumbrances forever?
>
> What are the five most important decisions that you can make right now about money?
>
> What resources and skills do you already have that will help you achieve your monetary goals?
>
> When you know you are overextending yourself, what will be necessary for you to stop immediately?
>
> What do you need to double or triple your monthly income within six months?
>
> What is the shift in your thinking, choices, and actions that will create financial freedom for you within two years?

Actions

> What can you do today to start creating a compelling financial future?
>
> What have you been putting off that you will take action on this week?
>
> What do you need to create a spending plan that matches your financial priorities?
>
> What can you do this week to assure your financial freedom?

Support

> Who can you emulate as a model of financial success?
>
> Who will you ask to help you reach your financial goals?
>
> How often will you review your financial goals and with whom?

To receive additional information and support, visit Kenneth D. Foster's Living Rich Coaching Community at www.PremierCoaching.com and www.GreatestYearEver.com.

SECTION 5

Questions to Empower Your Connections

LOVE

God works his magic through love, and the highest form of love is found by giving selfless service to others.
—Kenneth D. Foster

Have you deeply looked into the eyes of a newborn and felt the essence of joy this child brings into the world? Most of us can relate to the love we feel when in the presence of children. We come into the world filled with love and with an open heart. Right from the beginning children expand their love out into the world. From love we come and to love we go. What happens in between is what we discuss now.

As we grow and mature, we often succumb to the whirlwind of external beliefs and ideas out there and then slowly fall *away* from love. We might feel stressed or overworked, emotionally drained, unfulfilled, or lonely. What happens, then, is we become separated from the true nature of our souls, where the deeper wisdom within lies. We feel a void, cut off from the sunlight of our spirit, our truest feelings, and settle instead for shallow ones. Turn on any number of popular television shows and you will see painful dramas unfolding in any random episode. After all, when we separate ourselves from love, melodrama is the result!

When we start to experience discomforting feelings such as anger, sadness, resentment, bitterness, or hatred, it is many times a warning sign that we have stepped away from love. And a lack of love in one's life is the major cause of stress, anxiety, health problems, financial problems, neurosis, and the feeling of a lack of fulfillment. You may have heard the old saying, "Love is what makes the world go 'round!" Well, it is. It is what gives all of us the juice in life and the inspiration to carry on.

When we have fallen out of love with life, one reaction may be to search for it externally. We look for love in other people, places, or things. We think that maybe someone or something can actually give it back to us. The result is usually temporary happiness coupled with a deeper longing for love. In actuality, we are trying to find love "in all the wrong places." What I know to be true is that love is an inside job. Love is always *within* us. When we are feeling connected to our highest consciousness, we *are* Love. When we feel love inside our hearts and connect to our inner wisdom, we then radiate it outward. You can see it and feel it in persons who are connected to their source. The challenge most of us face is staying connected to love no matter what circumstances show up in our lives. The key to staying connected to love is through quiet introspection, meditation, reflection, and staying aware of our feelings. At any given point in time, we are feeling connected to love or disconnected to love. In other words, we are either connected to ourselves or not.

Did you know that without knowing and loving yourself you can never really love another? You may feel some temporary passion or lust, but true love is much deeper than that. The reason for this is simple. When you know who you really are at the core of your being, you will find and experience love. When you do, you will realize what you have been searching for is right within and you will stop trying to find it outside of yourself. Love is an inside job and is waiting for you to discover it.

Some people think that they can never find love. The good news is that we can learn to love ourselves no matter what has happened in our lives. The first step is acknowledging where in our lives that we feel a void. Then it takes willpower and a willingness to identify what's working in our life and what's not. This can be the biggest (and most important!) challenge in our lives. True love focuses back on the self and identifies the ways in which we need to change, develop, and grow.

As you look at what is working in your life and what is not, be sure to be gentle with yourself. Focusing on shortcomings and beating ourselves up isn't the way to bring in more love. On one of his visits to the United States, the Dalai Lama was overheard speaking to his interpreter, asking, "Why does it seem that so many people here in North America don't love themselves? Why do they give themselves such a hard time?" In his view, love for all begins with compassion for yourself. So when you look at what is happening in your life, notice what isn't working, and then focus on how to bring in more love in that area by asking powerful questions. If, for example, you don't feel any passion when you come to work, then acknowledge that you don't have any passion and ask, "What has to happen for me to feel great when I get to work?" or "What can I do today to feel passionate about my work?" or Who can I speak with who will support me in bringing joy back into my work?" Because love is active (and not passive), it is a continual process of opening your heart without condition. Acceptance of yourself is an essential piece of the process—identifying your errors in life, forgiving yourself and others, and then releasing it all to open yourself up.

So just how is it that we begin to get to know ourselves so that we may find love in our hearts once again? It is through the process of asking ourselves the right questions and deeply delving into love and what it means to us. We each have a responsibility to know our own love, bring it forth, and let it flow! When we go within and understand the depth of our own love, it is then that we may truly offer love to others.

The questions that follow will begin the process for you. Quiet yourself enough to clarify what love means to you and how you can be more loving toward yourself. Ask yourself the questions that will help you explore the deeper parts of yourself and find out just how much love is inside you. You may be pleasantly surprised, for love is limitless, abundant, and unconditional!

Love starts with giving, right here, right now. So give yourself the gift of love by taking the time to answer the questions in this section and start creating your own heaven on earth. Remember, those who know themselves know love and can easily give love. And when you give to yourself and allow yourself to bring to the world the gifts you've been blessed with, you will surely be blessed and feel love in return.

Love

Evaluation

When you think about love, what comes to mind?
Who do you love?
What do you love?
Who loves you?
Where have you succeeded in love?
What have you learned about love?
What takes you out of love?
Where have you experienced the deepest sense of love?

Vision

What types of love do you want to have in your life? (platonic, erotic love, soulful, unconditional)
What are the qualities of your soul mate?
What captivating moments are you ready to create?
What enchanting experiences do you want to experience?

Goals

What are your goals for having love in your life?
What goals can you set to have a loving and harmonious life?

Purpose

Why is love important for you to have in your life?

Commitment

> What are your commitments to yourself with regard to love?
>
> What are you committed to learning about love?

Blocks to Success

> What about love is challenging you?
>
> What thoughts do you consistently have that are getting in your way of having the love you want in life?
>
> Where have you been letting yourself down in love?
>
> When do you feel unloved?
>
> What do you need to rekindle or grow the love within your heart?

Quantum Thinking

> What would you have to recognize within yourself to experience more self-love?
>
> What does infinite love mean to you and how can you manifest this in your life?
>
> What will bring you unending love?
>
> What is love calling you to do differently?

Actions

> What actions are you willing to take to create lasting love in your life?

Support

> Who will support you in your quest to have more love in your life?

To receive additional information and support, visit Kenneth D. Foster's Living Rich Coaching Community at www.PremierCoaching.com and www.GreatestYearEver.com.

COMMUNICATION

Communication is the art of reason combined with compassion. As I listen deeply to your heart, mine begins to beat in the same sweet rhythm of understanding.

—Kenneth D. Foster

The way we communicate will lead to a successful life or a life filled with strife. We are communicating with ourselves and others every waking moment. We communicate through our body language, we communicate through words, we communicate through touch, and we even communicate through silence (have you ever had the experience of being in someone's presence and just feeling so in tune with that person that you need no words?)

Much of the time we do not bring our full awareness into communication. Life has become so fast-paced that we find ourselves just tossing off words or saying the most convenient thing, or not thinking at all about the quality of what we're communicating. Yet we know that both words and gestures can have an enormous impact on others. One of the worst effects of unaware communication is that the words we speak or the expression on our face can affect another person negatively and that person may carry the memory of those words for a long time. How often feuds arise in families or among friends, all based on something someone said 10 years ago—if you're the one who said it, *you've* probably forgotten, but the person you said it to, *hasn't*.

That's why it's so important to communicate mindfully and from the heart, not just the head. In my own life experience, I've uncovered what I feel are important keys to good communication. The first, and most crucial, is related to the mindfulness. We need to know what our *intention* is for the communication. Are we making a request? Are we giving feedback? Are we telling a joke? Are we speaking words of comfort or support? Are we being diplomatic? Are we being totally honest? Self-questioning plays a role in helping us clarify what our intent is. The old adage "Think before you speak" carries a lot of wisdom.

The second key is to be fully present to the other person. People can tell when you're distracted or not focused on them. If you don't give your full attention to the person you're talking with, that person will feel you don't particularly care about what you're saying or hearing. You will seem to be insincere. Being fully present to another is a way of showing respect for the *beingness* of another.

For communication to be highly effective, people need to feel safe. You don't want to feel that you're walking on eggshells every time you open your mouth. You don't want to feel that the person will immediately run out and repeat what you've said. You create safety through a sense of respect and an underlying trust between the communicators. You seek for ways to create a sense of connection and confidence. It might be a gesture, the way you make eye contact, your smile, your physical proximity to the person, your choice of positive and supportive words. To do all that, you need to totally let go of any judgment, criticism, comparison, and competition, and instead approach the other person in wholehearted support for where they're at.

Many of us are quite good at communicating what *we* want or what *we* intend, particularly if the issue is really important to us. We're less good at the receiving end of communication, the act of listening. There have been studies that show that the mere act of compassionate listening results in people feeling that they have been truly heard and understood, even if the person doing the listening doesn't say a word!

Hearing is about paying attention to words; listening is capturing the full essence of what is behind the words. The heart of listening is silent loving. When we let go of our agendas, such as thoughts of what we are going to do when the speaker is finished, or what we think the speaker *should* have said, we become present for the speaker in the moment.

By tuning in to more than the words, we actually start to hear on a much deeper level—a level deeper than we thought possible. Studies have shown that the *words we speak* represent only 7 percent of what influences other people's behavior. *How we use our voice* represents 38 percent of our influence, and an astounding 55 percent of our influence comes from *how we use our bodies* or *physiology*. If you are listening *only* to the words, you are missing a lot of the message.

Active listening is a *place we come from* rather than an *action we take.* The goal in active listening is to establish a soul-to-soul connection. We begin to actually sense where others are coming from, even without words being exchanged.

Growing up, most of us were seldom *fully seen and heard* by our peers, family, or authority figures. Many of us come from families that were struggling, striving, and surviving. Most people spend much of their lives in the *doing* state rather than the *being* state. As a result, we have not learned the skills necessary to be present for other human beings. By actively listening and being fully present with our attention, eyes, and actions, we can start to let go of our *human doing* state and become attuned to our *human being* state. To be there for another person without saying a word, just listening, is a powerful connection. This new dimension to listening honors people and is a powerful way to instantly connect to anyone at any time.

The heart of communication rests in being authentic—authentic in what we say, authentic in our gestures and body language, authentic in how we listen, and authentic in how we share. What distinguishes the word *authentic* from similar words like *sincere* or *genuine?* Webster's dictionary defines *authentic* as " . . . stresses complete sincerity, without feigning or hypocrisy." Being authentic, then, encompasses *both* sincerity and genuineness, and at bottom it means being *real.*

Authentic communication is the guidance we receive from our deep inner core whenever we relate to another human being. This guidance reflects our deepest values, convictions, philosophies, dreams, and beliefs—what is real and unique in us. It must be distinguished from the cultural conditioning, also known as *groupthink,* which are the collective beliefs and systems given to us by others, for example, parents, schools, relatives, and institutions. These programmed communication patterns are truly archaic. These speaking patterns contain many *shouldas, couldas,* or *wouldas,* and are guaranteed to constrict and suffocate the true self. This kills creativity and leads only to compliance and compromise.

An intimate relationship with ourselves is vital to the process of authentic communication with others. By connecting with your own authentic self, you will create spirited connections, soulful communications, and the vitality to connect with any individual, group, meeting, or organization. This is what authentic communication is all about! How do we learn this kind of authentic communication with ourselves? And how do we give this to others? The questions in this section are designed to do that—first by leading you to begin communicating authentically and respectfully with yourself, and then by opening you up to the mindful awareness of everything you communicate to others. True communication is never shallow or one-way. It is the sharing of our highest self with another's highest self. Communication is sacred. When practiced with forethought and love, it is the mark of everything it means to be human.

Communication

Evaluation

What is your confidence level with your communication abilities?
In what areas have your communications been less than adequate?
What areas of communication would you like to improve in?
Who are you not listening to?
What are you not listening to?
When communicating, to what extent are your inner feelings matching your outer expression?

Vision

What is your vision for the communicator that you want to become?
Where can you apply your current knowledge to become a better communicator?

Goals

What goals can you set to improve your communication skills and have fun at the same time?

Purpose

What is the value to yourself and your family when you become a better communicator?
Why will you become a highly effective communicator?

Commitment

What are your commitments concerning your communication to others?
What commitment are you willing to make toward yourself to be a better communicator?

Blocks to Success

What areas of your life are being limited by your current communication ability?
What is it costing you and others to communicate ineffectively?
What confining habits or ways of thinking are blocking your communications?

Quantum Thinking

To what extent do you live what you communicate?

What ways can you think of to communicate that are easier than your current methods?

What has to happen to make the information you want to communicate be more understandable to others?

Actions

What three action steps can you take this week to become a better communicator?

Support

Who do you most respect as a communicator and what qualities of that person do you embody?

What groups can you contact to teach you communication skills?

What key words can you type into Google Search or Yahoo Search to find some communication classes?

To receive additional information and support, visit Kenneth D. Foster's Living Rich Coaching Community at www.PremierCoaching.com and www.GreatestYearEver.com.

FAMILY

Daily review your decisions, comments, and behaviors,
then commit to modifying your choices to positively impact
seven generations into the future.

—Kenneth D. Foster

Our families of origin are our roots—parents, grandparents, siblings, aunts and uncles, and so on. And then many of us have a family we create on our own, where we leave our legacy: These are your spouse and your children. We also might have a family that is of our own choosing, composed of people who are not necessarily relatives, but whom we have deemed special enough to call family. There is a Lakota Sioux word, *hunkapi*, which means "making relatives" and refers to people becoming close to us who are more than just friends but not romantic partners. So family can be both something we are given, and something we create.

Regardless, we all have variations of family in our lives. While the thought of family might conjure up different things for each of us, the important thing, however, is what family means to *you* and how you see your role in the family.

Because families include such a wide variety of individual lifestyles, preferences, and values, it's not uncommon to find discord between its members. In *The Power of Intention,* Wayne Dyer says that we don't have to understand our family members to love and accept them, and this is where many of us get tripped up.

We often don't understand other family members and they don't understand us. And that's okay! We're all coming from a different place in life and while we may not always get each other, we can still choose to accept and love one another.

In our culture, it's often very easy for us to come up with critical thoughts of what doesn't work or what is wrong with other people . . . including the ones in our families. The more we concentrate and focus on what is beautiful or right with our families, the more we generate peace, love, and acceptance. It is up to you to do whatever you can to create an extraordinary family life.

We can either choose to continue to notice the things we don't like (thus, creating more of it) or focus our attention on what is good. By the way, focusing on the good and what people are doing right can be a lot of work. It is not easy maintaining a neutral mind when being around your family, but it does denote spiritual growth and maturity on your part. What a great example to set for the rest of your family. Focusing on the positive may well affect other members and might pique their curiosity too.

Have you ever heard of the expression "Pick your battles wisely"? When we are closely connected with another, it can be almost automatic to get upset about minor issues that wouldn't even make us flinch in another relationship. So decide about the battles that are worth getting involved in. For example, if you're noticing unruly behavior in your child that seems to be getting out of control, you may not want to nag that same child about putting the cap back on the toothpaste; it's not the most important battle of the moment! Plus, the calmer you are when dealing with family issues, the easier it is to make better choices, and you will probably like yourself better if you don't allow your emotions to run away from you on every little matter.

Celebrate family. It's what keeps our societies going. It's what bonds us. It's where we feel our connection. It's where we came from and where we are going. We each have the power to affect our families—positively or negatively. Make your choice carefully!

If you truly want to affect your family in a positive way, read on in the following pages and elicit the courage to ask yourself the tough questions. Remember; "Ask and You will Succeed." Once asked, make a list of positive actions that you will take and then take some immediate action. By the way, it is very easy to make a list and follow through if you will schedule the actions in your calendar and then firmly commit to accomplishing those actions.

Family

Evaluation

What are the most beautiful aspects of your family?

What is working with regard to your family?

What is not working with regard to your family?

What environmental changes would benefit your family?

In what areas does your family support you?

In what areas would you like your family to contribute to your life?

To what extent do you feel nourished and fulfilled in your family life?

Vision

What is the compelling vision you have for your family?

What adventures would you like to take with your family?

What is the greatest vision you can imagine for your family's future?

Goals

Is there a single change you are willing to make now that will enhance your family's well-being?

What goals can you set that will bring your family closer?

Purpose

What do you value most about your family?

Why is it important to you to create an incredible family life?

Commitment

What are you committed to doing to make your family life better?

Blocks to Success

What needs immediate attention in your family life?

Is there anything you have left unspoken to a family member?

What beliefs or messages did you grow up with that are having an impact on your family now?

Who in your family are you allowing to take away your energy and power?

Who in your family are you taking for granted?

Quantum Thinking

What can you do to foster cooperation, mutual respect, and support in your family?

What changes can you make that will affect your family in a positive way?

What gifts will you be leaving your family when you leave this earth?

Actions

What two actions could you take today to bring in more life and joy to your family?

What actions can you take to feel more nourished and fulfilled with regard to your family?

What can you do to surprise your spouse, children, or family to make them smile?

What could you do today to make your family life better for tomorrow?

Support

Do you need support to have a better family life?

What steps can you take today to get the support you need to have a great family life?

To receive additional information and support, visit Kenneth D. Foster's Living Rich Coaching Community at www.PremierCoaching.com and www.GreatestYearEver.com.

FRIENDSHIP

Each problem in life brings with it golden nuggets of
wisdom, which true friendships help us reveal.
—Kenneth D. Foster

Have you ever noticed how there are some people who give you energy, uplift your spirit, and make you want to be around them more? And on the flip side, there are also people who tend to drain your energy, bore you, and make you feel like you want to run! We are either nurtured by the energy people are putting out or repelled by them, so every once in a while it's important to step back and take stock of the people you choose to have in your inner circle.

A colleague of mine talks about her grandfather, Roland, a retired psychologist, who has been a mentor to her much of her life. Roland always told her about the importance of "pruning the shrubs" when it comes to friendships. "There is a season in life when certain friends fit perfectly," he said. "And then there are times when a friendship runs its course and it's important to honor that new direction in life."

Allowing certain friendships to wane can be difficult, but when there is stagnant energy in a relationship, it's time to reevaluate.

In deciding which friendships you would like to cultivate, it's important to understand what you want. A friend to share conversation? A friend to travel with? A friend to inspire you to succeed? A friend to understand what you are going through? A friend to create adventures with? Maybe it's all of them!

Think about what qualities are most important for you to have in a friend. The best way to attract that type of friend, of course, is to actually have the qualities that you would like to see in someone else. For instance, if you would like to have a compassionate friend, it would be important for you to have developed compassion within yourself.

It is important to note that like-minded people usually attract the same qualities to themselves. Like attracts like! Happy people generally attract happy people. Wealthy people generally attract wealthy people. Spiritual people generally attract other spiritual people, and so forth.

There is an exception to this rule. When a person has developed a quality to an extreme—opposites attract. An example of this would be a person who is an extreme giver who is looking for acknowledgment or some other way of filling himself up by always trying to please another. I have seen many people show up for coaching over the years who are unbalanced and attracting to themselves people they don't want to be around. They get rid of one relationship that didn't work, only to get involved in another person with the same qualities. This happens many times even if the client is aware that these types of relationships are destructive to them. They don't understand that there is a universal law, which says that we will attract to us what we need to heal.

Love (which is the essence of you) will attract to you and heal anything that is unlike itself. In other words, we are always looking—consciously or unconsciously—for mental, emotional, physical, and spiritual balance. If you are out of balance, you will attract to you someone who will create enough awareness in you (most often this is very painful) until you get the lesson.

In the example with the clients that attract takers to themselves, it has generally become very painful for them before they come to me. They generally don't have much time for themselves, and they feel overwhelmed because they are constantly giving their time to others. They primarily attract takers, who will take everything from their time and energy to their money.

The first step in healing this type of situation is by rigorous honesty—acknowledging what is not working, asking the right questions to get clear with the solutions and then daily actions until the person becomes balanced and breaks the cycle of attracting polar opposites.

Spend some time reflecting on who you are as a friend. What qualities do you bring to a friendship? What areas can you improve upon? What is important to you in the way you interact with others?

As social creatures, we are not meant to go through life alone! And friendships can add such a rich dimension to life. Friends help us through difficult times, cheer us on when we are working toward a goal, stand by our side when we need support, laugh with us, play with us, cry with us. Friends soften our rough edges.

I remember a time when I was wondering what to do next. I was living in a one-bedroom home in Encinitas, California. I was working in a job I didn't like, my money was running out, my career was on hold, and I really needed a friend that day. I decided to spend some reflective time thinking about how I had gotten myself into this situation and what I could do to get out of it, but I was at a loss to see the big picture of how I got into it and, just as important, how I was going to get out.

As I pondered my predicament, the phone rang. A good friend of mine, Eric, was on the line. He asked me some very enlightened questions about my skills, talents, dreams, and ambitions. Because of our friendship and the trust we had with each other, Eric was able to ask me some very personal questions with regard to my beliefs, dreams, and actions. By the end of the conversation, I had reconnected with myself, felt energized, and knew what I needed to do to create the life of my greatest dreams.

This would have taken me much longer by myself to do, if at all, but because my friend Eric knew the right questions to ask, my life changed dramatically and our friendship continues to grow.

And so, I recommend that you reflect very carefully when selecting whom you will be spending your precious time with. Friends are not to be taken lightly! They are the ones who help us in our journey through life and to be our best. Ringo Starr said it best when he sang, "I get by with a little help from my friends. . . ."

To help you think about your current friendships and what you want from those relationships, spend some time with the questions that follow. Make sure that your friendships are the ones that are right for you and support you in all your greatness!

Friendship

Evaluation

    What does a successful friendship look like to you?

    What have you always wanted in a friendship?

    What are the 10 greatest gifts you bring to a friend?

    Who is your most trustworthy friend and why?

    Who do you trust the least and why?

    What qualities of the person you trust the most are reflected in you?

What qualities of the person you trust the least are reflected in you?

In what ways do your friends influence your decisions?

Do you have friendships that you have outgrown? If so, why are you holding on?

Vision

What qualities matter to you most in a friend?

What is your vision for your lifetime friendships?

What would you like to do with your friends?

What would you like your friends to do for you?

Goals

What four most important goals can you set that will ignite your friendships?

Purpose

What do you value most about friendship?

Why is it important to you to feel deeply connected to your friends?

Why is it important for you to have fun in your friendships?

Commitment

What are you committed to changing in you to have outstanding friendships?

Blocks to Success

What is your greatest challenge regarding your friendships?

Which habits do you have that offend others?

What do you have trouble accepting in your friendships?

What do you regret or resent about your current or past friendships?

Quantum Thinking

What do your friends help you see or understand about yourself?

What opportunities do you create for your friends to experience their greatness?

What do you want your friends to remember you for?

What will have to happen for you to have the quality friendships you want and deserve?

What has to shift in you to become the friend you most desire to be?

Actions

What can you do today to bring real joy to your friendships?

What are you willing to give to have quality friendships?

What are you willing to give up to have quality friendships?

Support

Who do you know who has outstanding relationships with others who would agree to mentor you?

Where can you find support to create the friendships that you have longed for in your life?

To receive additional information and support, visit Kenneth D. Foster's Living Rich Coaching Community at www.PremierCoaching.com and www.GreatestYearEver.com.

RELATIONSHIPS

Inner reflection is fundamental to relationships. The more you understand your lessons, the more joy you will experience.

Kenneth D. Foster

It's safe to say that a goal for the majority of us is to have joyful, happy relationships that are harmonious in all areas of our lives. And, interestingly, there are two seemingly contradictory patterns in relationships: Like attracts like and polar opposites attract.

The great thing about both principles is that they help us learn about ourselves. With like attracts like, for example, if you're a cheerful person by nature, you may attract someone with a similarly optimistic outlook on life. If you're a person holding on to a lot of anger, you're probably going to attract a similarly angry person. In that sense, our relationships are a mirror of ourselves. Our relationships can tell us a lot about what we need to learn in life. In other words, if I struggle with my anger and I attract another angry person into my life, I see my anger *reflected* through them, which will show me my own tendencies and help me realize where I may want to make changes.

Now let's look at the other principle—the idea that opposites attract. Perhaps you are an unconditional giver and you attract someone who is a complete taker. Or you're a quiet, scholarly type who likes nothing better than curling up with a good book and you find yourself attracted to a person who loves outdoor adventures. The opposites attract idea gets very interesting when you cotton on to what's really going on. You see, the opposites attract idea is not really about opposites at all. It's about qualities in yourself that you're denying or unaware of. In other words, your opposite is in fact as much of a mirror to you as the like attracts like idea.

When we find ourselves attracted to a person who seems to have a personality dramatically opposite to our own or a person whose interests are very different from ours, it's because we unconsciously perceive that something in ourselves is missing, and so we project it outward onto another person. If you're the quiet book type of person and you fall in love with an outdoor adventurer, there is a part of you that wants more adventure in your life, but you may be scared to really try it. And the adventurer in being attracted to you is likely unconsciously longing to go inward into some quiet reflection, and admires your ability to be alone with yourself and a good book. If you're the giver and you're attracted to a taker, you need to look within yourself to see if there are areas in your life where you should be more assertive, when you need to be more of a taker at times, in the sense of standing up for your own needs in a relationship.

Both patterns—the like attracts like and the opposites attract—are mirrors reflecting you to yourself. You can learn from either of these patterns. But it takes reflection, self-questioning, and a willingness to look at the parts of yourself you may be uncomfortable with. Our relationships are often our greatest teachers.

Relationships offer us two main pathways. We can choose to see our relationships as opening us up to a more conscious awareness of ourselves and the other person. Or we can choose to turn away from the mirror aspects and pretend that everything the other person does has nothing to do with us. When you do the former, your relationship grows and flourishes. When you do the latter, you get stuck and then you numb this over as time goes on and you slip into routine and familiarity, which may feel okay on the surface, but can hide an inner discontent.

Not being willing to see ourselves in the relationship mirror is why so many relationships that start out on a high note, focusing on all the great things that brought the two people together in the first place, end up falling into a pattern of overfamiliarity and negativity. We allow ourselves to become critical of the other person. Habits that we once thought were cute now bug us. We stop respecting the other person and speaking in an honorable way. We cease doing the little things that bring them joy. After all, they'll always be there, so we take them for granted. Over a period of time, the relationship stops working.

I have had clients ask me what to do about a strained relationship in their life. To reignite that flame, we have to reignite the spark within *us*, and look at what's right within the relationship. And we can ask ourselves the question, "What is this relationship teaching me about myself?" These steps can help:

1. Acknowledge that there is a problem and your specific part in it.
2. Ask for guidance from your intuition.
3. Set your intention for what you desire and follow through with action.
4. Go within and ask what you can do differently in the relationship to bring back a spirit of harmony.
5. Surround the other person *only* in positive thoughts.
6. Release it to a higher source of energy (however you construe that for yourself as Higher Self or God or True Self).

You may be surprised to see a really big shift! It's all an inside job and we have to go within to get things moving.

One other thing to note about relationships is that sometimes they may no longer fit in our lives. The old saying goes that friendships come in and out of our lives at different times; they weave in and out during a particular season for a particular reason. We may need to choose to let go of a relationship. This doesn't mean anything other than that it's time to move on. If you do find yourself at the end of a relationship, feel gratitude for what that relationship has taught you. Even if the relationship was very negative, there is still a blessing there for you. At the very least, if you're leaving, it has taught you to release yourself from negativity. And know that there will always be a new relationship that comes along at just the right time!

As you take stock of your relationships, spend some time with the questions on the next few pages. These questions will take you within and help you clarify who you are, so that you can be sure you're attracting to yourself the right types of relationships.

Relationships

Evaluation

> What does your inner wisdom say about your current relationship?
> What has to happen to put respect back into your relationship?
> In what ways has your family upbringing influenced your relationships?
> What strategies do you employ to get others to fill your needs?
> What has been your biggest challenge in your relationships?
> Why did your past relationships pick you?
> What do you pretend about your relationships?
> What personal qualities have seduced you into unhealthy relationships in the past?

Vision

> If you could have any relationship you wanted, what specifically would it look like?
> What would make your relationship the greatest one ever?

RELATIONSHIPS 155

What are you searching for in your relationships? For example,
money, love, support, and so on.
What brings you joy in your relationships?

Goals

When will you awaken your soul and push yourself to find your
soul mate?
What three goals can you set that when you do, will attract your
perfect mate?

Purpose

Why is it important for you to have healthy relationships?
What are your five most important reasons for attracting a soul
mate?

Commitment

What behavior will you commit to changing in yourself to attract
your perfect mate?
What will you commit to in your next relationship?

Blocks to Success

Why have your relationships not worked out in the past?
What do you wish happened less in your relationships?
What are you tolerating in your relationships?
What is it costing you to be in your current relationships?
What does it cost your partner to be in a relationship with you?
In what areas of your relationships are you not asking for what
you want?
What feelings and behaviors serve as warning signs that you have
chosen a relationship that is not working for you?

Quantum Thinking

In what areas will you have to evolve to attract the perfect
partner?
What do you continue to believe that is stopping you from
having the relationship of your dreams?
What is your payoff for not having the relationship of your
dreams?
What is the connection between your spirituality and your
relationships?

Actions

What are three steps you can take immediately that will create more harmony in your relationship?

What kind of thinking and behaving on your part will attract to you the life partner you desire in your life?

Support

What information do you need to have to attract your perfect partner?

Who can support you in creating the relationship of your dreams?

To receive additional information and support, visit Kenneth D. Foster's Living Rich Coaching Community at www.PremierCoaching.com and www.GreatestYearEver.com.

SECTION 6

Questions to Promote Well-Being

SELF-CARE

Many have mastered people, places, and things,
but few have mastered themselves.
—Kenneth D. Foster

Self-care—our ability to take full responsibility of ourselves—is vital to a balanced, happy life. Very often, we find ourselves pulled in so many directions with so many demands on our attention that we feel frazzled and burnt out. I have to admit, I was not always good at self-care. I had to *learn* how to do it. It's actually a discipline. We are definitely creatures of habit, except many of the habits we form with our thinking tend to be disempowering—"I'm stressed out, I have too much to do, I don't like my boss, the kids are driving me crazy, I have to cut the lawn," and on and on.

But, you know, you always have a choice. For me, I chose the feelings of stress and being overwhelmed for quite a few years until, exhausted, I finally said to myself "Well, if I've chosen habits around being burnt out, how about if I create new habits around taking care of myself instead?"

Here is my own self-care discipline in my life today. In the morning when I wake up, the first thing I do is spend some time in meditation. Then I exercise, whether by walking or yoga or riding a bike or running. Another way I care for my body is through good nutrition. I'm a vegan most of the time, and I emphasize always putting healthy foods into my body. I'm not saying you have to be a vegan, only that it's a good idea to include fresh, nutritious foods in your diet. Too many processed foods or empty calories will dampen your energy.

I prioritize my work schedule every day so that I know what to expect for that day. And—*this is important*—I also allow for some extra time parameters because something will inevitably happen in the day that will knock the schedule off a bit. I may not accomplish absolutely everything I planned, but giving myself some leeway allows for that and prevents me from beating myself up over what I didn't get done.

In my home life, I create a beautiful environment. I fill my office and home with pictures and plants that create beauty, harmony, and peace. I reduce clutter. I get organized. I do one or two things every day to improve my home or office environment or to make things easier for the ones I love. I make time for my family—for my wife, my three daughters, and my three grandchildren. And it's important to me also to make time for my friends.

I close each day with meditation and I sleep incredibly well, knowing that I have given my best throughout the day. I celebrate what I have done well and I forgive myself for when I fall short.

Please don't think I am perfect at this. The self-care I'm describing to you now evolved over several years of me figuring out what was important and then finding ways to put it into action. It didn't happen overnight. Asking myself probing questions, such as the ones in this book, played a huge role. Am I getting enough leisure time? Am I creating time for my family and friends? How is my body feeling? Do I feel connected to my spirit?

Make a list of the habits that sabotage you. Maybe you have a habit of staying up too late so that you're tired in the morning. Maybe you have a habit of not returning phone calls and letting them pile up. Or maybe it's the opposite—you have a habit of always being on the phone and not getting to other things that are important. When you've identified the things that keep you from taking care of yourself, ask yourself, "What would I need to do to change this?"

Sometimes we get confused between the idea of self-care and being selfish. Selfish means it's all about me, my needs, my desires, and just steamroll over everyone else. But we're not talking about selfish when we're talking about self-care. We're talking about putting yourself first at the top of your list. Well, you may ask, isn't *that* selfish? Isn't that a me-first attitude? No, not at all. Here's the wisdom within self-care—unless you take care of *you*, you won't have the energy to take care of others. If you end up giving so much of yourself away that there's nothing left over for you, you're going to feel overwhelmed, tired, irritable, and resentful. That's the very opposite of self-care.

Ask yourself: What is draining me? What am I tolerating in my life that I shouldn't be tolerating? If you start looking at where the drains are in your life, you're going to find some answers. You're going to see that taking care of yourself is not just an add-on, it's actually at the center of everything you do for others. You can only be as good for others as you are for yourself.

Who is the one person you live with, day in and day out, from the time you are born until the time you die? It's yourself. *You* are the only person you live with every waking and sleeping moment. Your most important relationship—ever—is the relationship you have with your own soul and with your inner wisdom.

After you've become aware of what drains you and you begin to take some self-care steps such as getting more sleep, scheduling a massage, adding flowers or pictures to brighten your environment, going for a walk, whatever it is, then begin to think about what makes your creative juices flow. Look at some things you've always wanted to do but have been putting off. Put some of these things on your calendar. Take some steps toward doing them.

People often tell me, "This makes sense, but I don't have time to do the self-care thing or to indulge myself that way." But I'm here to tell you that there is no shortage of time. Time pressure is something we invent, something we choose, and it keeps us away from what's really important. I guarantee that when you start taking some time to care for yourself, you will free up your time. Suddenly you'll find that you're more productive, you actually get *more* done, and you don't feel irritable or tired. Don't wait until you're so burnt out that you're in a state of desperation or until a major accident or illness hits you over the head with a baseball bat and makes you slow down and take notice.

Today, do one small act of self-care and see how it feels. And then tomorrow add another . . . and another . . . until you've made self-care a habit. Use the questions in this section to measure your current level of self-care and write a whole new page in your life where stress and time demands will not get the better of you. Do it now. Self-care is the best preventive medicine there is, bar none.

Self-Care

Evaluation

What do you do to take care of yourself on a daily basis?

In your life, what needs less attention and what needs more attention?

What do you do that gives you the greatest feeling of self-care?

Vision

What features would you definitely include in a plan for your self-care?

What are the most effective ways you know to nurture yourself?

What will create serenity and inner stillness in your mind and
body?

If you could do anything you wanted without restrictions, which
would nurture your soul, what would it be?

Who do you admire who really takes care of himself and what
characteristics will you model?

Goals

What are your most important goals for self-care?

Are your goals regarding self-care aligned with your deepest core
values?

Purpose

What about self-care is important to you?

When it comes to self-care, what really and truly matters to you?

What will you gain by using your inner courage to take great care
of yourself?

Commitment

What self-care values are you committed to adopting and living
from today onward?

What has to happen for you to commit to taking extra care of
yourself?

Blocks to Success

By continuing what you currently do each day, what results will
persist in your life?

Which of your negative habits creates imbalance in other's lives
and your own?

In what areas of your life are you tolerating less than the best for
yourself?

What are your greatest fears and how are they holding you back
from taking care of yourself?

Where has not taking care of yourself paid off for you?

Quantum Thinking

What would happen if you lived a life with zero tolerance for
your own excuses?

What would your life be like if you gave up worrying about what
others say, think, or feel, and took more care of yourself?

Actions

> What new actions could you take on a regular basis that would make a tremendous difference in the way you feel?
>
> What three actions will you take this week to fortify your health care program?

Support

> Who do you know who will support you in achieving your self-care goals?
>
> What can you do to assure that you will maintain your self-care commitments?

To receive additional information and support, visit Kenneth D. Foster's Living Rich Coaching Community at www.PremierCoaching.com and www.GreatestYearEver.com.

HEALTH

Denying that doctors can cure, the mind can heal, or that faith can restore health misses the point, that the sole creator of everything works through his physical, mental, and spiritual laws.

—Kenneth D. Foster

Many people think of health as mainly having to do with their body being disease-free and fully functional. Actually, the origins of the word *health* give us a far deeper meaning. *Health* comes from the Old English word *hæþ* (pronounced exactly as the modern word) meaning "wholeness, being whole." Another Old English word, *hælan*, means "to heal." And yet another ancestor of the word *health* is the Old Norse word *helge*, which means "holy or sacred." The reason for this brief language lesson is not to be pedantic but rather to convey that health is far more than just having a functional body. It's a state of mind, heart, and spirit, along with the body, all adding up to a sense of wholeness.

I try to make my own health routines address this wide concept of wholeness. For my body, I eat fresh nutritious foods, starting by eating very light in the morning, having my heaviest meal around lunchtime and lighter again in the evening. I evaluate foods in terms of the amount of energy they provide and the level of nutrition they give to my body.

As I've mentioned elsewhere in the book, I'm a practicing vegan who puts a strong emphasis on the nutritional power of plant sources. You don't have to be a vegan if that's not your choice. There are several ways to eat healthy. If you decide to include animal food sources in your diet, you can make some healthy choices, such as eating more fish than red meat, eating leaner sources of protein than fat-marbled ones, and so on. The best rule of thumb to follow, no matter what your menu style is, is that fresh is better than processed, and less fat is better than empty calories.

I also include time each day for physical activity. I will usually walk, do a run, ride a bike, play tennis, water ski, or snow ski—all things that will promote physical movement. Research has shown that exercise is not only crucial for your body's health but also has an effect on your brain, enabling it to function more efficiently, quickly, and effectively. Exercise elevates mood as well and is one of the best remedies for depression, exhaustion, and burnout. It's also a great toxin remover. Regular physical activity has a strong effect on your lymph system—your immune system. Without exercising and moving your body, toxins tend to stay in your body. Exercise pumps them out.

On the mental side of my health routines, I choose very carefully what I read and absorb. I choose books, magazines, TV shows, and movies that will strengthen and empower me, as opposed to putting negative messages of violence or destruction into my brain. Just as you need to put healthy foods into your body, you need to put healthy thoughts into your mind.

Meditation is also part of my daily life. I meditate each morning and evening. It's been proven that meditation not only helps you focus, concentrate, and calm your mind and heart, it also reduces stress. It connects you to a source larger than yourself. It's this larger source, what some people call the superconscious mind, the Higher Self, the Divine, God, or a variety of other names, that helps you find the answers to your deepest questions, such as many of the questions in this book.

All of these practices contribute to my overall health. What I have found is that unless your body is damaged beyond repair, you can heal most things. If you have soreness in your back, that can be healed. If you have stiffness in your knee, that can be healed. Many people accept that aches and pains are just a part of life when in fact the opposite is true. By following a simple health routine, you can prevent many conditions that if left unchecked could eventually cause damage.

So, you might ask, if we all *know* that healthy eating, enough sleep, exercise, pursuing positive thoughts, and meditation are good for us, why do so many of us not *do* it? As a society we've become complacent. We've also become addicted to the idea of instant gratification. Very few people understand that happiness (and health is a big part of happiness) depends on some discipline and on keeping commitments to ourselves about what is important.

Let's take exercise as an example. Why do people not exercise? I think a lot of time people don't ask themselves the right questions. For example, do you value health? If you do value health, then the next question would be "What has to happen for me to have health in all areas of my life?" Once we know that physical activity is necessary for good health, the next step is to get some additional information on activities that might be of interest to you. Perhaps you decide you'd like to start walking. Look for information on walking—what kind of shoes you need, what distance you need to cover to get a good cardio workout from your walk. Perhaps you even look at hiring a walking coach, or if it's some other form of exercise such as strength training, you could hire a personal trainer or mentor to get you started. It's also great to find a group of people to exercise with, such as a group fitness class, dance class, or walking club.

And remember that everything you do to contribute to your health, you do for *you*, not for someone else. Very often, we become afraid to exercise or to change our way of eating because we think we have to end up looking like the models in magazines or like movie idols. *You* get to define how you feel. If you're giving yourself messages such as "I'm not good looking enough," "that guy is fitter than me," "I can't keep up with all those muscle types at the fitness club," and so on, you're simply stopping yourself from doing what you most need to do. Instead of focusing on your shortcomings, ask yourself what qualities you have that you feel really good about. Don't begin with a critical list of everything you feel is wrong with you. Accept instead and love the body you have and realize that no one, not even the movie star you most admire, has a perfect body. It's remarkable what airbrushing and makeup can do on the screen, so don't be fooled by thinking that the perfect celluloid image you see is what that person really looks like.

Even more important, stay focused on the idea that health is ultimately about wholeness. It's about treating yourself as the sacred being you truly are. It's not by criticizing yourself that you motivate yourself toward better health. It's by loving and accepting yourself, and feeling yourself to be the worthwhile person you already are. Loving yourself enough to give yourself what your body, mind, heart, and spirit need to be well will motivate you toward a sense of greater well-being in your life. Get to know yourself better and allow the questions in this section to guide you to a plan of health (wholeness) that is exactly right for *you*.

Health

Evaluation

How comfortable do you feel with your body and health?
What are your attitudes and beliefs about the food you eat?
How much exercise and sleep do you get on a regular basis?
To what extent do you like the tone, flexibility, and appearance of your muscles?

What do you consider the essential characteristics of sound health?

If you could really change your health, what would you change first?

What healthy habits are sustaining your health?

What new desirable health habits have you formed in the last six months?

In what ways do you release stress from your life?

Vision

What is your vision for the understanding of eating healthy foods and the digestive process?

What does your body need to thrive?

What are the most beneficial foods you could nourish yourself with today?

What foods could you eliminate from your life to feel better?

Goals

What has to happen for you to clearly define your health and fitness goals?

What are your top three health and fitness goals?

Purpose

What about personal health is important to you?

Why is it important to you to have a healthy body image?

Why will you accomplish your health goals no matter what?

Commitment

What are three commitments that you will make to keeping yourself healthy?

What new standards are you willing to set with regard to your health?

What can you commit to doing that will substantially improve your health and vitality?

Blocks to Success

What has stopped you in the past from having outstanding health?

In what ways are you shortchanging your health?

What causes you to become ill?

What habits are consistently taking you away from having great health?

Quantum Thinking

To what extent do you believe that your body is the temple for your soul?

What would your health be like without caffeine, alcohol, white sugar, and red meat?

What thoughts, if you persist in choosing them, will prevent you from having the health you want?

Actions

What are five things that you can do to create a healthier lifestyle?

What three activities do you enjoy that will oxygenate and energize your body?

What actions are you willing to take today?

Support

If you really want to become healthy, what would be the ideal resource to study?

Whom can you coach with to support you in accomplishing your health and fitness goals?

Whom can you partner with to support you with your health and fitness goals?

To receive additional information and support, visit Kenneth D. Foster's Living Rich Coaching Community at www.PremierCoaching.com.

ENERGY

Nourish your body with wholesome foods and your mind with soulful questions; then you will ignite the fires from within.

—Kenneth D. Foster

Science tells us that everything in the universe is made up of atoms, protons, electrons, waves, and particles. All of these phenomena are in motion, and we call this motion energy. There are several different forms of energy, including, but not limited to, kinetic, potential, thermal, gravitational, sound energy, light energy, elastic, electromagnetic, chemical, nuclear, mass, and quantum. They have been defined to explain all known natural phenomena. So, why is learning about energy important to us? Well, the quantum physicists are finding that Consciousness gives rise to energy in the Universe, which means that your thinking is dictating your energy levels.

Sri Daya Mata, a great Yogi, once said, "The power of the mind is the organizing and governing force behind all creation." There is much supporting scientific evidence to this statement, which is the subject of this section.

Take note of your thoughts. Do you realize that they occupy the greatest part of your existence? They belong to an interior realm that you must learn to rule since from your thoughts comes empowerment or dis-empowerment and a life well lived or a mediocre existence. When you keep the climate of your thoughts focused on high consciousness (being happy, being fearless, being joyful, being compassionate, being humble, being peaceful, and being agreeable) you have more energy, and when you focus the mind on the negative qualities of your life (what you didn't get, what you lost, what is wrong, worries, what you hate, and so on) you have less energy. You are free to choose your thoughts, so choose wisely. This is quite simple when you think about it.

We are feeling, emotional beings and our thinking dictates our emotions. When you think about what you don't want, you will feel that thought in your body, unless of course you have shut down your feelings. So, for most people who are connected to their feelings, what you focus on, you will feel. And, of course, what you feel will dictate what you do or don't do. When you feel down, most likely you won't feel like working. Get the point? So emotion is thought in motion and your emotions will play a large part in your life as to whether you have great energy and can accomplish what you want or not.

We spend our energy on all kinds of things in life. Some days, we might have boundless energy from the moment we wake up in the morning until we go to bed at night. Other times, we trudge throughout our days feeling wiped out without any trace of a spark of energy. Have you ever noticed how certain people and situations give you lots of energy and you feel jazzed in their presence? And then there are other situations and people, who after you've spent time around them, you feel zapped and like you can't wait to hit the sack. Why do you think that is? It is because we all carry an energy field with us and at any point in time the field is either filled with energy that is flowing through us, moving out quicker than it is flowing back in, or blocked from flowing in or out.

Since the very makeup of the universe is energy, energy never really goes away. Regarding energy itself, there is no *away*. But energy does circulate and has patterns of ebb and flow. Since we are creatures of free will, our own choices and actions have a direct effect on how energy presents itself in our lives.

So if you're feeling that your energy level is low, it's because you're making some poor choices about who you have let into your energy field or where you have focused your thoughts, and your energies will therefore be draining from you and getting in the way of the universal flow of life force energy through you.

What happens if you spend your energy in situations you don't really want to be in? You might feel powerless, frustrated, or caught in a cycle of anger. That is definitely energy not well spent! Or to put it another way, that's an example of your energy flowing out of you faster that it is coming in. As you focus on and give energy to where you believe you have been wronged, you have cut off the flow of energy into your energy field. Another way of putting this is that you have cut off the energy from the sunlight of your spirit. Haven't you noticed how drained you feel after you have been upset? Our reserves get used up when we don't spend our energy wisely—similar to what happens when we don't spend our time or our money wisely.

In my coaching, I encourage my clients to pay attention to their feelings and energy levels. If they feel low energy, I ask them to stop, go within, and ask themselves what is draining their energy. I ask them to pay attention to not only physical energy, but their mental and emotional energy, too. If they are feeling called toward something—whether it's toward a person, an idea, a place, or whatever—I ask them to assess whether this will empower them or disempower them; they will know most of the time if they take the time to check in. If I hear their voice come alive with energy I ask them to follow their aliveness, to follow the call. At the same time, when I hear my clients talking about an event that they feel like they should attend and there is complete flatness in their voice and in their energy, I get them to stop and check in with what's happening. It's obvious to me that there is low energy there, and there's a message for them in that feeling.

Energy affects what we attract into our lives, or to put it more accurately, energy often expresses itself through our attitudes. If we have a positive or negative attitude, it will influence our energy level and the vibration we emit. For example, if on a particular day we are in a bad mood, we'll be caught up in a low level of energy. We won't be emitting a high level of energy vibration. When our energy vibration is low, we're not attracting the things in our lives that we want to attract; we're attracting instead lesser things that aren't a match with our true selves.

This is all on a very subtle level, but we have all seen the results of a low energy vibration. We have all heard the phrase that misery loves company. If you sit around and complain or worry a lot, you will definitely attract lower energy circumstances and people into your life.

The opposite is true also: When we focus on positive thinking and look for what is good in our circumstances, our energy is always greater and our vibration increased, thus bringing the things into our lives that are more aligned with what we desire.

So, if you ever think that you have no control over the level of energy you're feeling, think again. You do have control. If you are feeling out of control, then start right this moment and ask yourself, "What has to happen for me to have great energy all the time?" Energy is all around you. It's your choice how you will use it. Take stock of your life and on the things you're feeding yourself. Begin with the food you eat. Are you nourishing your body with fresh foods (high energy)—lots of fruit and vegetables? Are you balancing the proteins and carbohydrates in your diet? Or are you filling your stomach up with processed foods, sweets, and empty calories (low energy)?

Then take a look at what you read or watch on TV. Is the content you're absorbing contributing to a high level of energy or a lower level of energy? This can be tricky, because if you're watching a crime drama, for example, the action on the screen may get your adrenaline going. But that increase of energy is actually negative energy because you're putting thoughts and feelings of crime and violence into your energy field. It's the equivalent of what happens when you eat a chocolate bar—you get an immediate spike of energy followed by an energy crash. On the other hand, if you're reading and watching positive content, you'll get more of a feeling of being in a flow, being more peaceful. Peaceful energy is powerful. Jangled energy is not.

Next, take a look at your relationships. Are you surrounding yourself with people whose energy is uplifting or are you a member of the "Oh, it's awful" club? Are you giving more than you're receiving? Or receiving more than you're giving?

Look for all the places in your life where your energy is out of balance, and resolve to bring your energy back to the point where you can feel in the flow. When you're in the flow of your own energy, rather than suppressing it or getting in its way, you'll be connected with the energy of the entire universe!

On the pages that follow are questions that will stir up some thinking about your energy—what you're bringing into your life, what you're emitting into the world, and what energy level you are currently experiencing and why.

Energy

Evaluation

> To what extent are you satisfied with your current energy level?
> What strategies do you use to maintain positive energy levels in your body?
> How much control do you have over the way you feel?
> What takes your energy level down when your life is going great?
> What increases your energy when life isn't going that great?
> When are you most comfortable with your energy?

What emotions take away your energy?
What thoughts do you have that increase your energy?
What emotion shows up when your energy decreases?

Vision

What is your vision to have great energy?
In what ways can you be more energetic and successful in life?
What qualities do people with high energy possess?
What is the best way to maximize your energy level?

Goals

What are your three top goals to increase your energy?

Purpose

What compelling reasons could you give for wanting to increase
your energy level?
If you don't increase your energy level, what will your life be like
in five years?
Why is it really important for you to increase your energy?

Commitment

What are you committed to avoiding in order to have high
energy?
What are you committed to learning about increasing your
energy?
When are you committed to having more energy?

Blocks to Success

What parts of your life have you sacrificed by not maintaining
high energy levels?
What scares you and drains your energy?
What emotional states do you consistently feel that drain your
energy?
What are you tolerating that may be blocking your energy?
When have you doubted your ability to increase your energy?

Quantum Thinking

Where does your energy come from and how can you increase it?
What would have to happen for you to have all the energy you
desire?

What would have to take place in your mind to have unending
energy?

What role do depressing thoughts play in your energy, and how
can you transcend them forever?

What has to happen for you transcend the feelings of weariness
and discouragement forever?

Actions

What five actions can you take to raise your energy level?

Knowing that anything is possible, what can you change immediately about your energy?

Support

How can you learn to face any situation in your life with
maximum energy?

Who can support you in increasing your energy?

To receive additional information and support, visit Kenneth D. Foster's
Living Rich Coaching Community at www.PremierCoaching.com and
www.GreatestYearEver.com.

ANGER

More than personal or national enemies, the greatest
challenge to man is himself. By remaining ignorant to
the cause and cure of anger, man becomes his own
worst enemy.

—Kenneth D. Foster

So, just what does anger have to do with success? Everything! A life filled with anger is a life of violence and chaos, one in which peace and tranquility are strangers. It is a life led by resentments, where blame is a constant companion. Anger is the cause of broken homes, broken dreams, and broken lives. An angry life is an unsuccessful life.

When resentment-born anger is left unchecked, it can harden into impenetrable barriers, emotional defenses that separate us from the ones we care about most. If you live your life from behind these walls, finger-pointing and blame will be so rampant that you become incapable of taking responsibility for your actions. Dreams and love wither and die.

Despite the dire consequences of living this way, why are so many of us so angry? Is it because the rewards we seek are not immediate? Is it because we face challenges to our most passionately held convictions? Is it because we've experienced abuse or bullying when we were younger and unable to defend ourselves and we've let it simmer inside us for years? Or is it because we've inherited some long hard-wired instinct we cannot overcome? It may be impossible to know all the reasons, but that doesn't mean we can afford to ignore this sometimes paralyzing force.

Anger can be an intense emotional state, a sense that you are being antagonized by some*one* or some*thing*. But it can also be a chronic condition, and for many, it simply becomes a habit. Sometimes we humorously call perpetually angry people curmudgeons or hotheads or we laugh it off as having a short fuse, but this belies the debilitating effects of living life from a place of anger. Anger is generally rooted in feelings of frustration and helplessness, envy and jealousy, the belief that you are unable to attain what you want and the fear that you will lose what you have.

Anger also results from having our boundaries crossed. When we're angry, we sense a violation of some kind. It could be a violation of our body, such as in a physical assault. It could be a violation of the mind such as being told to shut up when we're expressing an opinion. It could be a violation of the heart when we experience rejection. It could be a violation of the spirit when someone poisons your spirituality with ideas of guilt and unworthiness.

Sometimes anger, in response to a violation, is healthy. Numbness is very often a reaction when a person has experienced a pattern of abuse.

The person shuts down feelings as a protection against the devastating feeling of being violated. Often, in counseling, when a person becomes aware of all the repressed anger over the abuse, that's the beginning of the healing process. Feeling anger is not a problem; *acting* out of anger *is* a problem.

Anger, like all human emotions, is an energy, and we can decide what to do with this energy when we feel it. We can use it to lose our temper, to get back at someone, or to destroy ourselves. Or we can use it to speak up for ourselves, to draw a boundary, to admit to others and to ourselves that a situation or a pattern is distressing for us, and that we are choosing for it to stop.

In that sense, anger is very tricky. It can be the signal that tells us we need to check our boundaries. It can also be the whirlwind that spins us right out of control. The lesson of anger in our lives is first to discern what is causing us to feel angry, then to decide what to do about it in an assertive, but not out-of-control way, and finally to gather the strength to let go of the anger. Holding on to anger after it has served its purpose of alerting you to a situation you need to pay attention to is destructive. Anger is meant as a sometime emotion, not as a way of living.

Anger almost always hurts the angry person more than the object of the anger. The person who made you angry may not even *know* he made you angry; even if he does, he has likely moved beyond whatever feelings of responsibility—or lack thereof—he had, while you continue to stay stuck in your anger. You cling to the anger as if it were a precious jewel. You replay the circumstances that gave rise to it over and over in your head. You fixate on how you were right and he was wrong. In engaging in an endless hypothetical argument, you have given this person power over you.

When we continually focus our thoughts on negative emotions of ourselves or others, we have planted a seed of suffering. And when we don't know how to handle our own suffering, we spread that suffering to anyone within earshot. Those who have offended, or who hold this power over you, cannot cause you to feel perpetually angry *unless you let them*. Don't let them. First, admit to yourself that you are angry. Then, see if you can isolate the factors that trigger this anger, that keep its embers glowing. After you have identified them, consider your values in determining how and why the situation really set you off. What is important to you? In the grand scheme of your life, what is it that *really* matters?

Now that you have put your anger into this perspective, can you let go of it? Are you ready to forgive the offense and move on? Or do you feel an airing of your grievances is required first? Once you have reflected on the nature of your anger and come to some enlightenment, you must take action to defuse it.

Letting go of anger is an ongoing process, and one that may never fully be complete. However, by understanding the root cause of your anger and its triggers, you can gain control over it, lessen its power to influence your feelings and behavior, and potentially even find something positive looming beneath its surface.

Our anger is never really about something external. Rather, our anger is our *reaction* to an external stimulus. So, as we accept ourselves as the *cause* of our own anger feelings, we can gradually turn the anger into feelings of peace, love, and compassion. To begin the process, reflect on the questions that follow in this chapter. Think about the last time you were angry and what patterns you have seen show up in your life.

Connect with any anger you might feel now in your body; your heart, your stomach, your gut. Learn from your past experiences and release yourself from any anger that currently holds you prisoner. *Only you have the power to free yourself.* Not only will you feel lighter physically and mentally, but when you learn something about yourself from anger, believe it or not, you can make it your ally and thus another foothold on your climb to success.

Anger

Evaluation

For how long have you carried anger?
What is the cause of your anger—the real cause?
What underlies the cause of your anger?
What do you get out of being angry?
Where has anger served you in the past?

Vision

What is the ideal way for you to deal with anger?

What would your life be like without any anger in it?

How will you treat others when you heal your anger?

What will be the greatest thing that happens to you when you are no longer carrying anger issues?

Goal

What is the most important goal that you can set around healing your anger?

When will you transcend your anger?

Purpose

What is it costing you to hold on to resentments?

If you do not deal with your anger, what will it ultimately cost you?

Why do you want to let go of your anger?

Commitment

What are three commitments you will make that will keep you calm in all circumstances?

What can you commit to doing that will substantially improve your serenity?

Blocks to Success

What or who do you resent?

What is the source of your greatest fears that contribute to your anger?

Where has your self-esteem been lowered because of your anger?

Where do you feel your anger has wounded you?

Quantum Thinking

What has to happen for you to forgive yourself for past mistakes?

What can you do to completely erase the petty things that are bothering you?

What would it take for you to release your anger forever?

What can you do to find serenity on a daily basis?

Actions

When are you really going to get help to release your anger issues forever?

With regard to letting go of your anger, whom can you forgive
today?

What actions can you take today to let go of petty annoyances?

Support

What groups offer anger support in your area?

Who do you know who has gone through anger issues and can
support you to move past yours?

Who can you meet with on a weekly basis to help you transcend
the anger habit?

To receive additional information and support, visit Kenneth D. Foster's
Living Rich Coaching Community at www.PremierCoaching.com and
www.GreatestYearEver.com.

HOME ENVIRONMENT

Evaluate your environment. Do the things around you empower you and move you toward success—or do they disempower you and hold you back?

—Kenneth D. Foster

The idea of home is often one of the most precious values we hold as human beings. It's no accident that many of our most beloved sayings are about home—"Home sweet home," "Home is where the heart is." When we feel comfortable with something or someone, we often say that we feel at home. Since the sense of home and being at home appear to be so important to the human psyche, take a few minutes to reflect on what home is for you and how you have set up your current home environment.

To me, home is a place that reflects my values. It's a sacred safe space. It's a place of love, a place of fun and laughter. It's a place of rejuvenation. It is a place of friendship and family—a place of beauty.

A healthy home environment is also clean, well lit, well ventilated, free of toxins, pests, and dangerous gases. It is dry, clean, comfortable, and affordable. In other words, home is a safe place where you can feel at ease, mentally, physically, spiritually, and emotionally. It's the place where you nurture your spirit.

It doesn't matter whether your home is large or small, whether it's a tiny studio apartment, a bungalow, a mid-size house, or a mansion. Every living space can be a reflection of peace, harmony, and beauty. Today, I own a large home, but twice in my life I had let go of most of my material possessions. The last time this happened I was living in a one-room place in southern California. In that tiny studio apartment I had beautiful plants and beautiful pictures. I had my computer and desk set up and organized. I put new carpet on the floor. I made sure the apartment had lots of fresh air and sunshine. In this tiny studio I felt joy every time I was home.

The reason I make sure my environment reflects a positive outlook is because my experience has taught me that if you wake up in a place that's really dismal—gray, cluttered, gloomy—it's going to have a definite negative effect on your mind and emotions. If you're living in a place that you don't feel good about, it's going to be difficult to start each day by saying "I'm glad to be alive and I feel good."

For most people, their environment is stronger than their willpower. It will affect how you think and feel. That's why it's so crucial to create your home to be as beautiful as possible. If you wake up each morning and see your favorite pictures, if you're well organized and there's no clutter, and you've created an environment that you're happy to be in, it's going to be much easier for you to stay in a happy place in your mind and heart.

You may ask, "Well, how can I do that, especially if I'm living with someone? What if I have different ideas than my partner does about what creates the harmony and beauty you're talking about?" Yes, it's certainly the case that when you don't live alone, you do have to take your partner's (or your roommates') tastes into account. But it's nevertheless possible to create an environment that's pleasing for all of you.

Here's how I worked out that challenge in my own life. When my wife Judy and I were first married, we looked at all my stuff and at all her stuff. I didn't really like a lot of her stuff and she didn't really like mine. We had quite different tastes. So we said to each other, "Well, you know, there are millions of pictures in the world, millions of pieces of furniture, thousands of different carpets, different colors of paint and different flowers, why don't we try an experiment? Let's do this—let's just bring into our home things that we both love and let go of the rest."

Believe me, this didn't happen overnight! It was a process. But once we had made the commitment to create an environment we both would find appealing, we gradually made choices that reflected both of us. We had our share of struggles and differing opinions about what to let go of. But slowly, we created our home environment with pictures, furniture, carpets, paint, and art we both love. So today when you walk into our beautiful home, there's a sense of peace and harmony.

One important aspect of creating a harmonious home environment is that it's constantly evolving. Every morning shortly after meditation, I ask a simple question. "What can I do to improve my home today?" Then I look around to see if there are things I can do that day to make our home environment better. One day, it might mean repainting a room. Other days, it's just picking up a few things. Just imagine the impact it will have on your home if every day you have done something, some small action, to make your home more beautiful. That's 365 opportunities for easy home improvement that will have quite an impact on your home, overall!

Use the questions in this section to reflect on your home environment. And if you haven't done this in a while, set an intention to create a home that really reflects you and your values. How do you feel when you're at home? Do you feel nurtured? Do you feel peaceful? Do you feel joyful? Do you want green plants that connect you with nature and purify the air? If you're an animal lover, do you want a companion animal in your home? If so, what animal do you resonate with? Are you a dog, cat, or bird person?

Do you feel like you'd want to invite your friends into your home? If not, then ask yourself what would have to happen to spiff up your home so you feel good about it. By the way, here's a quick remedy for home improvement—if you want to change your home environment, especially the clutter, just throw a party—because you'll almost certainly clean up beforehand! And you'll clean up again afterward!

How about setting up a goal to create the most beautiful home you have ever lived in? Or set up a goal to update your home and create a new design that is more aligned with you. Once you set your goals, then answer the questions in this section and be prepared to make some real and lasting changes. All of this can be a lot of fun, and you will have great satisfaction when you have completed a home environment makeover.

Home Environment

Evaluation

On a scale of 1 to 10, what rating would you give your home environment?

What do you enjoy most about your home?

What do you least like about your home?

What needs less attention and what needs more attention in your home?

What is perfect about your home right now?

What do you want to change about your home?

Vision

What specifically would be your ideal living environment?

What would it take to create the home environment of your dreams?

What do you want more of and less of in your home life?

What will it take for you to create a really supportive, nurturing home environment?

What can you do today to bring more love into your home?

What has to happen to create more beauty in your home?

Goals

What are the three top goals that will transform your home in the next two weeks?

Purpose

Why is it important for you to have a great home environment?

What is the price you pay for not having the home environment of your dreams?

Commitment

What can you commit to doing in the next two weeks to improve your home environment?

Blocks to Success

What in your home have you outgrown?

What could stop you from creating the home environment of your dreams?

What has to happen for you to transcend any blocks to creating an incredible home environment?

Quantum Thinking

What in you needs to change so that you can create your perfect home environment?

What has to happen for you to feel fulfilled in your home?

If you knew you could make your home life more fun, what would you do?

Actions

What daily actions will you take over the next two weeks to transform your home environment?

Support

> Who do you know who can help you design the home environ-
> ment of your dreams?
>
> Who do you have in your life who has a flair for design and can
> help you beautify your home?
>
> What web sites or magazines can you look at to get design ideas?

To receive additional information and support, visit Kenneth D. Foster's
Living Rich Coaching Community at www.PremierCoaching.com and
www.GreatestYearEver.com.

SECTION 7

Questions That Will Give You More Joy

FUN

The foolish look for happiness outside of themselves; the wise find it within and have the utmost fun playing their part in life.

—Kenneth D. Foster

"Remember, this is meant to be fun," I recently said to my client when she was preparing for a big presentation. I made that comment to her because she was completely stressing herself out and immersing herself in the details, forgetting that this upcoming presentation was an aspect of her job, which she loves. But unfortunately, somewhere along the line, the fun had gone out the window.

Has this ever happened to you? We get so caught up in the doing and in the details, that we have disconnected ourselves from any sort of fun whatsoever! And after all, isn't it our choice as to whether or not something is fun?

In the dictionary, *fun* is described as something that "provides amusement or enjoyment." But what is fun for one person is not necessarily fun for the next person. So you've got to decide what fun means to you. Have you ever made a list of what is fun for you? What brings you happiness and joy? This is a good time to do it, because the more focused attention you put on bringing more fun into your life, the more you will have. Can it be that simple—*yes!* Of course you have to not only plan, but you have to follow through with your commitments to yourself. The first step is to go within and ask yourself what can you do to have more fun? In the busyness of today's world, it's just too easy to lose sight of those things that are fun and bring us joy.

If you are in a place where you are feeling down or are dwelling on the thoughts that there isn't much fun in your life, then it is time to start laughing again. Laughter is our body's greatest natural medicine. Numerous studies show that laughter releases chemicals in the brain known as endorphins. These natural brain chemicals make us feel good. They relax our body and ease our heart. A life without laughter is an unhealthy life. Having fun is as necessary to us as eating!

So why don't we laugh more? Well, for many, it is because we are taking ourselves way too seriously and we are looking at what is wrong with our lives instead of focusing on the blessings we have in our life. If this is you, then make a decision today to start focusing on what is funny. Why don't you come up with 10 ways to bring more laughter into your life? Use your mind in a positive way to bring in more laughter and I guarantee you will find it.

My client decided to intentionally add a little humor into her presentation. In her preparation, she actually started to have more fun with the process because she deliberately reminded herself to plug in some fun!

Kids are great at having fun. That goes without saying. But then something happens as we grow older, advance in our careers, buy a house, settle down, raise a family, and so on. The fun does not have to stop, nor should it! In fact, this is precisely the time in life to be more aware of creating fun because if we don't do this, we end up falling back into the mundane chores and responsibilities in our lives. And if that's okay with you, then there is no need to read any further. However, since you have chosen to pick up this book, then I think it is safe to say that you are not willing to settle for a mediocre life!

Take a break from your daily routine and assess how you are doing at bringing fun into your life. Identify the opportunities that you could increase your fun quotient with for the sake of your joy, your sanity, and your overall well-being. If this is at all difficult for you, just observe children, for they can be our greatest teachers.

Children don't have to think about having fun; they just do it. They play with a deep innocence and focus on the moment. They never stifle a laugh or ponder the risk of looking silly or foolish. Their joy comes from the depth of their soul and is genuine, pure, and primal.

If you need some other help getting started, try a funny movie or listening to a comedian. Read a humorous book. Tell some jokes to your friends. Do something zany. For example, if you're a person who lives mostly by a disciplined routine and you plan everything carefully (which is great for success), find some time when you'll decide to break those rules and just be spontaneous for a time. Let's say you decide to go away for a weekend. Instead of planning where you're going to go, just get in your car and go where your intuition tells you to go. Do something on the spur of the moment!

I recently climbed to the top of the highest mountain in the lower 48 states, Mount Whitney, with four friends of mine. On our first night, we camped beside a beautiful waterfall. We had been hiking for six hours, so all of us were a little spent. Then, out of nowhere, spontaneous laughter overtook us as we all looked at one another and asked, "How did we get in the middle of the Sierra Nevada Mountains climbing the tallest peak?" "What were we thinking?" asked one of my friends. That one question set off a wave of laughter, because it was obvious to all of us that we had a long way to go to the summit, and if we took ourselves too seriously we would never make it. Our laughter that day helped us deeply connect with one another. It enlivened our spirits and helped us not think about how tired we were or how far we had to go. By the way, we did make it to the summit of Mount Whitney two days later, laughing all the way to the top and back.

It feels good to laugh and to have fun. It makes all aspects of life a whole lot easier. Spend some time with the questions listed here and connect with that innate human desire to laugh and have fun. Remember that each of us has the power to create more fun in our life. That choice is yours. Are you ready to laugh more and bring in more fun?

Fun

Evaluation

    What is your definition of fun?
    Generally speaking, what amount of fun are you creating?
    What areas of your life do you want to bring more fun in?
    When have you had the most fun in life?
    What do you do that brings you the most fun?
    What are the fun things that you like to do?
    When are you most playful?

Vision

    What would have to happen for you to create the best (birthday, Christmas, holiday, and so forth) ever?
    What is the funniest thing you can imagine doing?
    What tips would you give a friend in your situation to have outrageous fun?
    How would your life be different as a result of having more fun?

Goals

    What are three important goals that you will set and accomplish to have more fun?

Purpose

What about having fun is important to you?

What is your primary objective for having more fun?

What are your top five reasons for having more fun?

Who do you know who would benefit by you having more fun?

Commitment

What are you willing to give or give up to have more fun?

What do you need to have in place to totally commit to having more fun?

Blocks to Success

In the past, what has stopped you from having the fun you deserve?

Who have you let stand in the way of your fun?

When do you benefit by not having fun?

Quantum Thinking

What are you willing to move past to allow more fun in?

What would you need to believe is possible for you to have outrageous fun?

What do you need to have in place to have consistent fun in your life?

Actions

What are the action steps that you can take to have more fun in your life?

Support

Who is the funniest person you know who can support you in having more fun?

To receive additional information and support, visit Kenneth D. Foster's Living Rich Coaching Community at www.PremierCoaching.com and www.GreatestYearEver.com.

HAPPINESS

Find that which is full of life, vibrant, and joyful;

it is there you will realize happiness.

—Kenneth D. Foster

My six-year-old granddaughter, Ella, walked into my office one day and sat in my chair. She had heard me coach clients over the years, so I asked her, "Would you like to be the coach today and bring in some wisdom?" She looked at me and then sat up straight in the big chair and I could tell that she was ready to be the coach. Then she asked me, "What would you like to talk about today, Grandpa?" I said, "Happiness."

Then she asked me, "Does your mommy and daddy ever get upset with you, and then you don't feel happy?" Playing along with her, I said that they do get upset with me and it makes me feel sad, so I asked her what she suggested I do. "Grandpa," she replied, "You need to think happy thoughts!" When I asked her what kind of happy thoughts, she simply said, "Any kind of happy thoughts—just think happy thoughts and then things will get better for you." What wisdom from this little person!

Did you know that the cells in your body all have memory and respond to your moods? The vital life force in the cells actually adjusts to your positive or negative moods. They align with your thoughts. When we are happy, all the cells in our bodies are flowing with life energy. When we are sad, the cells become devitalized and drop life force energy. If you worry and are stressed out, you can turn a great day into a deep depression. If you consistently agonize and put pressure on yourself, you can change your hair to gray and stress your heart to the point where blood flow is restricted. Is this any way to live?

Especially when things don't go our way, many of us focus on what we don't have, what's missing, what dreams didn't happen for us, or what's wrong. Very seldom do we take all of that energy and focus on introspection in a good sense to help us grow, develop, improve, and change. For us to be happy, we must focus on happy thoughts. To do that, we need to direct the mind by asking questions that will empower us. Questions like "What will create real happiness for me?" or "What has to happen for me to be happy in this moment?" Then take immediate actions to create the happiness inside of you.

Be aware, though, that we may have put up some roadblocks along the way to our own happiness. We might have unhealed expectations about how things should have been. For example, maybe our childhood wasn't how we expected it to be. Oprah Winfrey is a great example of this, as she had a childhood that was quite troubled. She learned from it, however, and turned it around for the good. There is a part of each one of us that is longing to learn and move past any wounds, no matter how deep, to tap into the unending happiness that is right within our own consciousness.

So first off, we need to assess ourselves with powerful questions in the different areas of our lives—health, wealth, spiritual, career, social—where are we happy and where are we not to get clear on where we want to improve. You get to choose what you want to focus on: the problem or the solution. Most of us stay focused on the problem way too long and feel like a victim. But when you choose to notice the problem and then focus your creativity and attention on the solution instead, you become empowered.

Happiness is like an iceberg—most of it is lies within, while a small portion is revealed on the surface. Fill yourself up with the abundant joy of happiness-filled thoughts deep within your heart. Nothing external can create permanent happiness. The new house, car, relationship, or the job—the happiness these may create is temporary and fading. So we must learn to create lasting happiness from within. We need to know ourselves and ask ourselves the enlightened questions of what really does bring us happiness. Because when we focus on what will bring us lasting happiness, our happiness will expand.

Now it's time to ask yourself the all-important question of what will bring you lasting happiness. Then move on to the questions that follow on the next few pages. After all, happiness comes from a deep spiritual place and we need to go deeper within to find out who we are at a soul level and what brings us joy. Going back to the wisdom of my granddaughter, when you think happy thoughts, things will get better for you!

Happiness

Evaluation

On a scale of 1 to 10, with 1 being dismal and 10 being off the chart, how happy are you?

When are you the happiest?

What takes away your happiness?

When you feel happy, what manifests in your life?

What triggers happy emotions in you?

What has been the happiest time in your life?

Vision

What does a consistently happy life look like to you?

If you could spend one year in perfect happiness, where would it be?

What makes you truly happy and engages you so deeply that you aren't aware of time passing?

Goals

What are your happiness goals?

What are the most essential goals you can set around being happy?

Purpose

Why are you choosing to create more happiness in your life?

What will more happiness bring you?

Why is it important for you to have more happiness in your life?

Commitment

What three things will you commit to doing that will actually bring you lots of happiness?

Blocks to Success

What is limiting your happiness?

What price have you paid for choosing unhappiness?

What fears are blocking your happiness?

What are the experiences in your life that create unhappiness for you?

Quantum Thinking

What will bring you permanent happiness or bliss?

Where does happiness reside in you?

What thoughts can you consistently focus on to bring you happiness?

If you consistently focus on what makes you happy, what problems will you release?

How can you experience quantum leaps in having more happiness?

Actions

> What can you do right now to create more of your ideal life?
>
> What has happened today that has enhanced the quality of your life?
>
> Starting today, what can you do to create a happy future?

Support

> Where can you find a happiness coach?
>
> Who are the happiest people you know, whom you could meet with on a regular basis?
>
> What group could you contact to support your happiness goals?

To receive additional information and support, visit Kenneth D. Foster's Living Rich Coaching Community at www.PremierCoaching.com and www.GreatestYearEver.com.

REST AND RECREATION

*Nourish your body with pure foods, pure thoughts,
and plenty of rest to ignite the fires from within.*
—Kenneth D. Foster

Let's face it, our society promotes, encourages, and rewards multitasking and busyness. You don't have to be a rocket scientist to see people out of balance• everywhere! We're running around from meeting to meeting, talking nonstop on our cell phones. We're sending text messages like crazy and we're addicted to e-mail. We're on the go, grabbing fast food, not making time to exercise, and our minds are constantly busy thinking about what's next. At the end of the day, we can't seem to shut it all down. We become overwhelmed, overstressed, and our immune systems are overtaxed. All we want is a little peace.

So why don't we just go out and get it? We don't because the environment is stronger than most people's willpower. The influences around us are pushing us to work more, do more, have more, and be more . . . whatever the cost. That cost, though, is very high! Without rest and relaxation, we end up with symptoms of disease in all areas of our life: Our bodies get old before their time, our minds become feeble, our relationships stop working. We are living in homes that we don't want to be in and working in jobs that we don't enjoy.

Have you ever noticed that it takes several days for many people to calm down while on vacation? Why is this? It is because many people have not learned how to control their thinking. They have not found the pause button in their mind to turn off all the noise. It doesn't have to be this way, but we have to learn how to use our minds better. It is our thoughts that determine our feelings, and our feelings will most likely determine the actions you take or don't take.

Take time to start using your mind to create what you want in life. The questions in this section focus your mind in the direction of rest and relaxation. You don't have to wait until the next vacation to feel relaxed. You can start feeling relaxed right now. As mentioned earlier in the book, "The Answers are in the Questions you ask." So how about asking a question like "What is it that would really bring me rest and recreation today?" You will get the answer as long as you keep asking the question. For many of us, we feel a respite when we go on vacation. But what if you could have that feeling every day? For people who live a balanced life, this is their reality.

When you're balanced, your body and mind are renewed on a daily basis. Relationships become fresher and more immediate. Your work gets more inspired. This happens when you use the power of your mind to focus on creating rest and recreation daily, and it happens by asking yourself questions that will guide you and point you in the right direction. For example, you may want to ask, "What are three things I can do today to relax my mind?" And again, once you ask the question, answers will come.

Maybe the answer will be to meditate, read a book, go for a walk, take a bath, or go outside to admire the stars. Rest and recreation calms our bodies and calms our minds; it's the place of renewal that we all yearn for. When our mind and body are renewed, life gets better because we are able to make better choices that are aligned with our true spirits.

Speaking of vacations, we seem to be pretty good at planning our vacations. We take the time necessary to make all the preparations and get all the details in order. What would happen if we took great care of our daily lives, just as we do with our vacations? What if we planned every day to have a mini-vacation as part of it? Maybe that mini-vacation is a walk in the sunshine, maybe it's meeting a friend at the gym for a squash game, maybe it's a time stretched out in an easy chair where you just allow yourself to daydream, maybe it's a nap, maybe it's playing with your children or grandchildren. Whatever it is, don't deny yourself the pleasures that will come to you as rest and relaxation. Sometimes spending time doing nothing is the most productive thing we can do!

Think about what, specifically, renews you. It will probably be different from what renews your spouse or what renews your boss. Make a list and also jot down what it is that you're honoring within yourself when you take the time to renew. Then keep that list handy because in the moment of stress and feeling of being overwhelmed, it can be extra difficult to think on the spot about ways to get out of that place and the underlying importance of doing so. Do this homework ahead of time and you will see the rewards pay off!

Also, the questions that follow will do a great job of helping you get started on your path to new and improved rest and recreation. Enjoy spending time with these thought-provoking questions!

Rest and Recreation

Evaluation

What creates most of the stress in your life?

When you feel overwhelmed, what is the cause?

When do you feel most rested?

What does it mean to you to recreate?

How often are you taking time to recharge your batteries?

Vision

What does perfect rest and recreation look like to you?

What brings you the most rest?

What comes to mind when you think about recreation?

What do you love to do when you are playing?

What are your top five places where you would like to vacation?

What is your greatest vision for rest and recreation in your life?

Goals

What goals will you set to have more rest and recreation?

What date will you accomplish these goals by?

Purpose

What might your health be like in 10 years if you don't get enough rest and recreation?

What does it cost you and your family when you don't have enough rest?

What are the five most important reasons for you to get sufficient rest and recreation?

Commitment

What is the pledge you will make to yourself to have enough rest and recreation from here on out?

Blocks to Success

What do you feel stops you from getting enough rest and recreation?

What did you learn from your family that is blocking you from getting the rest you deserve?

What beliefs are driving you to the point of overtaxing your body and mind?

Quantum Thinking

How can you recreate so that you are relaxed all the time?

What beliefs are you willing to move past to bring in more rest and recreation?

What would you need to know, without a doubt, to have more rest and recreation in your life?

Actions

What are you willing to give or give up to feel more rested and relaxed?

What specific action steps will you set regarding rest and relaxation?

Support

Who can you emulate who has a balanced life, is consistently well rested, and takes time for recreation?

Where can you get the information you need to have more rest and recreation in your life?

What groups can support your rest and recreation goals?

To receive additional information and support, visit Kenneth D. Foster's Living Rich Coaching Community at www.PremierCoaching.com and www.GreatestYearEver.com.

TIME

Modern thinking says that we lose time when we aren't multitasking and doing things quickly, yet the truth be known, when we slow down and focus on the task at hand, we gain productivity, satisfaction, and happiness.

—Kenneth D. Foster

There is a saying, "Time is of the essence." The essence of what, exactly? A reasonable interpretation of the maxim is that everything we do in this physical life is carried out through the medium of time. How we use our time is crucial to achieving our dreams.

I recently asked one of my clients what results she was currently getting in her business. She replied that she was experiencing some improvements but that things were not unfolding as quickly as she would like. She had a goal of increasing her monthly income to $10,000 from $5,000. I asked her what was going on in that gap between $5,000 and $10,000. We began to explore her use of time. It turned out that she was caught up in just being busy. She spent time on the computer, reading the newspaper, and chatting to others on the telephone. But this wasn't *focused* time. This wasn't getting organized in the morning and taking specific actions to lead her to her goal. She was allowing herself to get sidelined by extraneous influences that were detracting from the essence of what she wanted to accomplish.

To address this situation, we developed a set of questions for her to ask herself every morning. The first question I asked her was, "What will you accomplish today that will lead you closer to creating $10,000 a month?" The next question was "As the CEO of your company, what are your priorities for the day?" Then I asked her, "Why is this important to accomplishing your goals, keeping you on purpose and on point?" Finally, I asked, "What must you believe in order to create $10,000 a month, and what three things could you focus on today to move in this direction?" These questions helped her pay attention to the way she was using her time. She went on to develop some of her own questions, which supported her in staying focused until she accomplished her goal.

What I find with time management is that as a society we've got so much going on in our lives, we find ourselves on information overload. Technology has sped up the pace of life. It's the information age, and there are so many people who want you to have their information. If you're not really clear about *your* direction, you're going to get off track time and time again. On the physical level, time is finite, so if you're wasting time, you're creating a lack of success in your life.

What are some of my own time management strategies? As the CEO of my company, I have a lot of projects coming my way. I make a list of all the projects I'm involved with. From there, I prioritize the tasks involved in the projects as A, B, or C. A is something I will complete today. B is something I will complete a bit later, likely in the next few days. C is something I'll delegate. With both my A list and B list, I block time out in my calendar. If I need to expand time for a certain project, I'll allow for that when I'm filling in the calendar. Having an appointment or task appear in writing on my calendar makes it real. It's a reminder to me to keep the commitments I make to myself regarding my business.

I also allow for time interruptions, because, let's face it, there are always going to be interruptions. I used to be upset in the past when people or situations interrupted me. I asked myself, "What would have to happen when I am interrupted so that I not feel upset?" I realized that I needed to allow time for interruptions and to understand that it's just part of life. Now when someone does call me unexpectedly or walks in on me when I'm in the middle of a task, I'll listen briefly to what he has to say and then politely let him know that right now I'm staying focused on my project. I'll ask him if we can arrange another time to talk.

Sometimes, there are emergencies. If there's a family emergency, I'm going to handle it right then and there. In my business, if something comes up that only *I* can handle and it has to be dealt with immediately, I'll do that. But, generally speaking, I set time boundaries for myself and my business. I let others know what I'm doing. For example, if I'm doing a recording session, I let my assistant know. If I'm working at home, I let my wife know. Informing staff or family of what I'm doing is a way of asking them to assist me in holding the time for the task. In this way, the people around me support me in creating the boundaries. In your own life, it's just a matter of saying, "I'll be busy with this for the next hour, and so unless it's an emergency, please don't interrupt me. I'll check in with you in an hour."

At the level of physics, we know that measured time is a concept created by humans to determine where we are in the space-time continuum. Our ancestors, many thousands of years ago, measured time by the sun and moon and by the cycle of the seasons. In the modern world, we've invented clocks and time zones. We've lost much of the natural connection between time and nature. We live in a 24/7 busy world. So while it's important to implement good time management strategies, we need to also realize that there is this *fabricated* aspect of time that can run away with us if we let it. Most of the world's great spiritual traditions have the concept of staying in the present moment. The fact that this insight occurs in virtually every great world religion indicates that we instinctively know that there is wisdom in the now. But often being habituated to time periods keeps us in the past or catapults us into the future, and we forget where we are right now.

Let's say that a business associate walked into your office three weeks ago and said something that upset you. Today, you see that person again and you find yourself remembering what she said three weeks ago and you feel upset all over again. Where are you? You've gone back to the past. If your thoughts and emotions are focused in the past, you're not able to be completely in the moment with the person right now. So whatever she might be saying *now*, you won't really hear the message. It's the same with the future. Let's say that you have an upcoming meeting in five days with a colleague whom you've experienced as difficult to deal with. You may be ruminating for the next five days on all the ways you plan to protect yourself from getting upset. You spend time worrying about that meeting. Where are you? You've gone into the future. If your mind is busy anticipating the future, you're not going to be present for the tasks you've got right now. There is a difference between *planning* for the future and worrying about the future. There's a difference between contemplating the past to help you understand it and brooding about the past in the sense of not letting go of what happened.

All time is happening in the moment. So as we choose our actions and our thoughts moment to moment, this is where our focus will be. If we allow ourselves to be fully in the present, that's where we find energy, creativity, and intuition. That's where we find our wisdom. That's why so many meditation practices imported from the East to our stressed-out West emphasize allowing yourself to rest your consciousness in the present.

Some people think that time management and being in the present are contradictory. But they're actually part of the same ebb and flow of life. We definitely have to know how to use our time wisely, and that takes planning. We also have to know how to be fully present to our own experience, moment to moment, so that we can savor all that life brings to us. Use the questions in this section to explore your own relationship with time. You'll begin to understand how time really does relate to your essence.

Time

Evaluation

What shows up when you are managing your time appropriately?

What do you waste time on?

What is the number one time-management skill you are currently benefiting from?

In what ways do you use time to serve you?

How are you giving away your time?

Vision

Where do you plan to spend most of your time in the next five years?

What is your strategy for creating more time for yourself?

What is the best use of your time?

What new and significant time management skill could you begin using?

Goals

What are the most important goals you can set to become a highly effective time manager?

Purpose

What are your highest priorities concerning the use of your time?

How do you feel when you are not managing your time effectively?

Commitment

What are you committed to accomplishing with regard to time management?

Blocks to Success

What is the payoff when you do not manage your time effectively?

In what ways do you limit the time you have to spend on what you really love doing?

When does it serve you to limit the time you spend doing what you love?

What amount of time do you spend living in the past or future?

How are you disempowering yourself by making poor time management decisions?

What do you fear about time?

Quantum Thinking

What results would you expect by managing your time more effectively?

What do you need to be more proactive and influential in mastering your time?

What has to happen in your life for you to be in the flow with time?

Actions

What are five effective ways you could create more time for yourself?

What action steps can you take to improve your time management skills?

Support

What courses can you take to better manage your time?

Who would be a great role model for you in using your time effectively?

What is the top time management book that will really help you deal with time issues successfully?

To receive additional information and support, visit Kenneth D. Foster's Living Rich Coaching Community at www.PremierCoaching.com and www.GreatestYearEver.com.

TRAVEL

Set your intentions to live life fully. The saddest summary of a life is looking back and wondering if I only would have, could have, might have, or should have. Honor and cherish your greatest dreams by manifesting them.

—Kenneth D. Foster

Ahhh . . . travel. Most of us crave or want some sort of travel in our life. We long for adventure and the feeling of being alive. We want to visit distant places, experience cultures different from our own. We want to see Earth's beauty. We want to meet new people and have new experiences. Travel offers us this opportunity.

For much of my adult life, I stayed within approximately a 10-mile radius of my home and very seldom traveled outside of that area. My consciousness at that time was limited: I had a small group of friends, I went to and from work, I came home and turned on the TV, I ate lots of processed foods, I didn't read much and my thoughts were very similar to my parents, even though I thought I was very different. One might say that I had a small life. But in my world, I didn't realize there was another way! I didn't realize the vastness of the world because I had a very limited view of myself and what I was capable of. Therefore, I limited my world.

When I finally began to travel once or twice a year, I noticed that I had a sense of peace about three days into it. This happened consistently enough to make me realize that travel was something that very much agreed with me. When I came back home, I had more awareness and a sense of connection with myself and with the world. I noticed that I had an expanded consciousness about what was going on in the world, I got to experience different foods and cultures, and I had a new way of looking at life. In essence, *travel changed my perception of who I was and who I could be in the world.*

We are certainly creatures of habit! And these habits can easily keep us stuck in a rut. It takes a bold act to break out of a rut. Travel is a perfect way to do it! Travel gets us outside of our comfort zone, and most of us learn something when we are in a new or different environment: Our senses come alive, our eyes become opened in a new way, we begin to feel more, and we find ourselves focusing on things that are different, weird, or beautiful.

If you are sitting in a familiar environment right now and there is a window near you, look out. What do you see? Is it a tree, a building, a lake, a field? How would you describe it? When we're in familiar environments, things simply stay familiar and we oftentimes miss the beauty that is right under our nose. When we travel, however, we look out our window and see a tree that is just like the one back home, but this time we say, "Wow!"

Have you ever noticed that when you come back from traveling, you might feel exhausted as though you've been caught up in a whirlwind? Have you ever asked yourself how you can travel and feel completely refreshed when you arrive back home? Is this even possible?

Well, I can tell you that over the years I have learned about what I call *conscious traveling*. This is a form of travel that leads to extraordinary experiences. Conscious traveling involves asking yourself the right questions before, during, and after your trip, so that you create experiences that nurture your spirit and expand your life. Conscious travel forces us to tap into our deeper wisdom, and explore our intuition, which in turn supports our journey into the richness that life has to offer. As a result, our spirit comes alive, vibrating joyfully throughout each day in our travel experience.

I realize that it is easy to get all excited about travel plans, hurriedly pack your bags, and get out the door. This is what most people do. But wait! There is a better way. When you take time to plan out your experience and decide what it is that you *really* want from your travel—mentally, emotionally, physically, and spiritually—you bring a higher consciousness into practice. Ask yourself: Do I want rest and relaxation? Do I want to meditate near a stream? Which tours will enliven my spirit? What is it that I feel called to see? Where have I always wanted to go? Remember, the richness of the questions you ask will determine the richness of your trip.

So, to create meaningful and conscious travel, be intentional about it. Go within and ask yourself what would bring you true happiness in your travel. And then develop a plan to make that happen! If you're traveling with others, be sure to involve them in the process. Let them know your intentions and find out theirs as well to eliminate confusion and pre-conceived ideas and to ensure a great time together.

And don't forget the joys of going off the beaten path! Don't just be a tourist, but try instead to see the culture you're visiting through the eyes of the people who live there. Go to some of the restaurants where the locals hang out. Talk to some of the local people about their lives. Be curious, but not disrespectful. Greet each difference you encounter with an open and curious mind.

As you prepare for upcoming travel, get started with the questions that follow. They will be a great catalyst to launch you on your journey. Remember to venture within *before* you venture out!

Travel

Evaluation

Have you traveled where you want to go?
What about travel do you enjoy?
What do you dislike when you travel?
What benefits do you receive from traveling?
Where have you most liked traveling to?
What are the five most important things you have learned while traveling?

Vision

Where in your heart do you long to travel?
Whom would you like to travel with?
What is the most exquisite travel experience you can imagine?
What are the top five exotic places that you will be traveling to?

Goals

What are your travel goals?
What is your strategy for fulfilling your travel goals?

Purpose

Why is traveling important to you?
What are the five most important reasons for you to travel?

Commitment

What are you committed to accomplishing with your travel goals?

Blocks to Success

What has stopped you from traveling when and where you want?
What is your excuse for not traveling where you want?

Quantum Thinking

What will take your travel experiences to a world-class experience?

What travel opportunities are available to you now?

What arrangements do you need so you can travel more in your life?

Actions

What are three steps that you can take immediately to start accomplishing your travel goals?

What are three steps you can take this week that will guarantee your travel goals become reality?

Support

Who do you know who has traveled extensively who can help you accomplish your travel goals?

What is a great travel company or agent that can help you with traveling to where you want to go?

To receive additional information and support, visit Kenneth D. Foster's Living Rich Coaching Community at www.PremierCoaching.com and www.GreatestYearEver.com.

SECTION 8

The Only Remaining Questions

THE ONLY REMAINING QUESTIONS

To know the thoughts of God is to know how

to succeed in life.

—Kenneth D. Foster

As you've been pondering the questions in this book and writing your answers in your journal, you've developed the powerful habit of intro-spection. Congratulations! This is one of the most important skills you can develop to have a successful life. The ability to self-reflect and ask the right questions along with the understanding of how to tap into your intuition and wisdom will change the course of your life.

As we move further into the twentieth-first century, it's going to be more and more imperative to draw upon our inner wisdom and be mindful of the skills of decisive thinking, intuition, inspiration, creativity, and integrity. The world needs influential questioners—with inspired answers to solve the troubles of the twentieth-first century and lift the consciousness of our planet. By continuing to live in the super-conscious questions, you will continue to find the answers—the answers that are right for you, your family, and your community to create a compelling destiny.

As we arrive at the end of the book, and as you scan back through the 34 categories and their relevance to your life, I leave you with a final five questions. The answers to these questions will come from the collective energy of all the questions you have asked yourself and answered in the process of using this book. Think of these as the Big Picture that has come together from the kaleidoscope of your own wisdom awakened by the many hundreds of questions you've been exposed to here.

The path to your success is in your hands. May you live well and long and continue to be blessed with a deepening of wisdom, enthusiasm for life, joy to nurture your spirit, resolve to manifest fulfillment, and abundance to have the means to be of great service to others. And remember this simple phrase: Ask and You Will Succeed!

The Only Remaining Questions

Based on what you have learned about yourself:
    Who are you?
    What is the purpose of your life?
    Where truly does the source of your power reside?
    Who do you know who would benefit by asking these questions?

THE APPENDICES

APPENDIX 1

To further strengthen your habit of introspection to keep the momentum going on your path to success, here are some questions to ask yourself each morning. Feel free to choose among the questions and combine them as you feel moved to. Let the energy of the Morning Questions create your day—today and every day to come!

Morning Questions

If I had one month to live, would I choose to do what I am about to do today?

What will I accomplish today that will make me successful?

What incredible memories do I want to create today?

What have I been thinking that has created my life the way it is?

What am I committed to believing so that I may have an astonishing life?

What three things can I focus on today to move me in the direction of my dream life?

What will I do to make a difference in someone's life today?

What are the healthiest foods I can put into my body today?

What book or tape will I read or listen to today to inspire me?

What am I truly grateful for in my life today?

How will I exercise today to increase my energy and strength?

How do I feel after asking and answering these questions?

APPENDIX 2

To quicken your understanding of yourself and see reality clearly, it is important to review your day and perceive truth from the veils that hide it. You will not discover your real path to success unless you develop the habit of reviewing your day to discover your true nature.

Evening Questions

Overall, what worked for me today and what did not?

What goals did I accomplish today and what did I put off?

In what specific ways have I grown today?

On a scale of one to ten, what was the quality of my life today?

How did I spend my time (constructively, useful, meditation, prayer, focused, wastefully)?

In what ways could I better spend my time tomorrow?

What good habit did I strengthen today?

What was my predominant attitude (moody, angry, critical, worried, fearful, courageous, willing, thoughtful, generous, truthful, hopeful, cheerful, loving, joyous)?

Which of my attitudes or moods empowered me and which ones disempowered me?

What new belief will I focus on tomorrow to stay in my power?

What did I learn today?

What will I apply more earnestly tomorrow no matter what?

APPENDIX 3

Quotes for Success

VALUES CLARIFICATION—*"Right choice is a function of living our highest values; so, too, it is the key to a life well lived."* **Kenneth D. Foster**

LIFE PURPOSE—*"Great minds choose a purpose for their lives that inspires greatness in others."* **Kenneth D. Foster**

MISSION IN LIFE—*"Your life cannot be repeated. It is now or never, so find out who you are, what your heart longs to achieve, and then sail away from safe harbors and explore your greatest dreams."* **Kenneth D. Foster**

SPIRITUAL—*"In the garden of your heart, find the Master of the universe, for He will help you water your dreams with love, your challenges with fearlessness, and your activities with joy."* **Kenneth D. Foster**

CONTRIBUTION—*"Service is the way we say thanks for all that has been given to us."* **Kenneth D. Foster**

BELIEFS—*"When a man stops thinking in limited terms, he starts knowing unlimited success."* **Kenneth D. Foster**

PERSONAL DEVELOPMENT—*"Personal growth starts with your thoughts, for no one experiences anything that they don't hold first in their mind."* **Kenneth D. Foster**

BOUNDARIES—*"Success is determined by a person's character, and character is determined by the promises you keep to yourself and others."* **Kenneth D. Foster**

CLEANING THE CLUTTER—*"Order doesn't start with an outer action, but with a vision of symmetry that is set up from within."* **Kenneth D. Foster**

ORGANIZATION—*"A calm and organized mind creates a calm and organized life."* **Kenneth D. Foster**

DREAMS—*"To set yourself free, you must give yourself permission to dream bigger than you have ever dreamed before."* **Kenneth D. Foster**

GOAL SETTING—*"No one can predict how great your life will be, not even you, until you choose to be great by setting goals and achieving them."* **Kenneth D. Foster**

COMMITMENT—*"If you want to accelerate your rate of achievement, you must ask new questions, explore new commitments, and take daily focused actions until success is achieved."* **Kenneth D. Foster**

SUCCESS—*"Environment is stronger than most people's will, but faith coupled with resolve will conquer all."* **Kenneth D. Foster**

QUANTUM BREAKTHROUGHS—*"To know the thoughts of God is to know how to succeed in life."* **Kenneth D. Foster**

CAREER—*"To be on fire with the passion of purpose puts joy in one's work."* **Kenneth D. Foster**

BUSINESS—*"When your energy, creativity, and enthusiasm becomes unending, you have found the secret to business success."* **Kenneth D. Foster**

LEADERSHIP—*"There is no shortage of leaders today—they are everywhere. But there is a shortage of great men and women who empower others, are compassionate, and serve the greater good."* **Kenneth D. Foster**

MONEY—*"The answer is in the questions you ask, and the magnitude of your questions will establish the size of your answers. So ask multimillion-dollar questions if you want to get multimillion-dollar answers."* **Kenneth D. Foster**

LOVE—*"God works his magic through love, and the highest form of love is found by giving selfless service to others."* **Kenneth D. Foster**

COMMUNICATION—*"Communication is the art of reason combined with compassion. As I listen deeply to your heart, mine begins to beat in the same sweet rhythm of understanding."* **Kenneth D. Foster**

FAMILY—*"Daily review your decisions, comments, and behaviors, then commit to modifying your choices to positively impact seven generations into the future."* **Kenneth D. Foster**

FRIENDSHIP—*"Each problem in life brings with it golden nuggets of wisdom, which true friendships help us reveal."* **Kenneth D. Foster**

RELATIONSHIPS—*"Inner reflection is fundamental to relationships. The more you understand your lessons, the more joy you will experience."* **Kenneth D. Foster**

SELF-CARE—*"Many have mastered people, places, and things, but few have mastered themselves."* **Kenneth D. Foster**

HEALTH—*"Denying that doctors can cure, the mind can heal, or that faith can restore health misses the point, that the sole creator of everything works through his physical, mental, and spiritual laws."* **Kenneth D. Foster**

ENERGY—*"Nourish your body with wholesome foods and your mind with soulful questions; then you will ignite the fires from within."* **Kenneth D. Foster**

ANGER—*"More than personal or national enemies, the greatest challenge to man is himself. By remaining ignorant to the cause and cure of anger, man becomes his own worst enemy."* **Kenneth D. Foster**

HOME ENVIRONMENT—*"Evaluate your environment. Do the things around you empower you and move you toward success—or do they disempower you and hold you back?"* **Kenneth D. Foster**

FUN—*"The foolish look for happiness outside of themselves; the wise find it within and have the utmost fun playing their part in life."* **Kenneth D. Foster**

HAPPINESS—*"Find that which is full of life, vibrant, and joyful; it is there you will realize happiness."* **Kenneth D. Foster**

REST AND RECREATION—*"Nourish your body with pure foods, pure thoughts, and plenty of rest to ignite the fires from within."* **Kenneth D. Foster**

TIME—*"Modern thinking says that we lose time when we aren't multitasking and doing things quickly, yet the truth be known, when we slow down and focus on the task at hand, we gain productivity, satisfaction, and happiness."* **Kenneth D. Foster**

TRAVEL—*"Set your intentions to live life fully. The saddest summary of a life is looking back and wondering if I only would have, could have, might have, or should have. Honor and cherish your greatest dreams by manifesting them."* **Kenneth D. Foster**

THE ONLY REMAINING QUESTIONS—*"To know the thoughts of God is to know how to succeed in life."* **Kenneth D. Foster**

WHAT'S NEXT

If you would like to find out more about creating success in all areas of life and continue your adventure into the world of self-discovery, please join Kenneth D. Foster by signing up for his blog, success coaching, workshops, and learning at:

asksucceed.com
greatestyearever.com
sharedvisionnetwork.com
Email: contactus@asksucceed.com

Kenneth would also like to invite you to join the Shared Vision Network, a professional development network for soulful entrepreneurs. Founded in 1991, the Shared Vision Network is dedicated to empowering members to grow highly profitable businesses and realize their full potential.

Activities include creating and sharing your vision, training from nationally recognized speakers, authors, and business educators, dynamic networking events, wealth-building educational workshops, an online business community, discussion groups, mastermind groups, success coaching, and an online business university with resources geared to help you improve in your professional and personal life.

Membership is available to entrepreneurs who are committed to excellence, service to others, and making a difference in the world. Use the discount code ASKSUCCEED to get your first month for just $9.98 at: sharedvisionnetwork.com.

WE ARE LISTENING!

We would love to hear how this book has affected your life and the lives of those around you. We encourage you to share your insights and stories. If you have a tip or a quote that you would like to share, please send it to us. With your permission, we will put these insights and tips on our blog or web site to help others grow in their lives. Please e-mail us at: contactus@ask-succeed.com or visit our web site www.asksucceed.com.

WE ARE GIVING!

Kenneth is currently offering high quality bonuses in excess of $1,000 for purchasing *Ask and You Will Succeed*. You are also eligible to receive a discounted fee for a personalized Success Coaching session. This is available to everyone who has purchased this book and is serious about improving, changing, or developing his life to the fullest extent. This is a limited offer and we reserve the right to cancel this offer at any time. To take advantage of this offer, go to www.premiercoaching.com and get started today.

WE ARE SUPPORTING!

To grow your vision and live an extraordinary life, you will need to ask bigger questions, dream bigger, turn your dreams into goals, resolve to accomplish those goals, and take focused actions every day. You will also need a support team. To this end, we recommend you find a coach or mentor and a networking group. To do life alone is boring, dull, and glum! Go to sharedvisionnetwork.com and grow your business by networking your way to success with people who are making a difference. Use the discount code ASKSUCCEED to get your first month for just $9.98.